"In this work, which I have had the pleasure of sharing with students for the past five years, I have been able to see first hand the power and vitality of a philosophical play. In Is It All Relative? Pierre Grimes has created three characters, Harry, Joseph, and Elea, who represent archetypally the drama of contemporary intellectual life. The drama centers around a challenge given by a fourth archetype who has been unfortunately absent from the contemporary discussion—the pagan philosopher. The Greek's Challenge, as it is named in the play, challenges the three characters (and the reader) to confront the prejudicial beliefs that block them from examining their own life and the world with the clarity of unhindered vision. In the play and its appendix you will be introduced to the classical models for reasoning and exploring ideas that will transform the way you see history, religion, science, philosophy, and most especially, yourself."

Robert Apatow, Assistant Professor of Humanities
Art Institute of Southern California

"Reading this challenging book, one is brought to truly see and understand the subtle ways in which we have as a society and as a world come to accept the incredible mediocrity which results from seeing and living in the world as relativists. In addition, the reader will profit from seeing how analogies, metaphors, and similes are the keys to seeking out truth. The reasoning covered in this slim volume addresses issues which affect education, the environment, government, and personal insight. I recommend it to anyone who truly wants to challenge personal beliefs about themselves and the world. This is not dry academic philosophy, but a living example of how to reason and communicate without ambiguity."

William Gilbert, Lecturer in Critical Thinking
California State University, Long Beach

IS IT *Really* ALL RELATIVE?

Is each person truly entitled to his or her own opinion? Even though many profess this view, do they really live their lives according to it?
Is such a life even possible?

Is it all Relative?

Is It All Relative?

Pierre Grimes

HYPARXIS PRESS
COSTA MESA, CALIFORNIA

Hyparxis Press
2172 Pacific Avenue
Costa Mesa, CA 92627-3912

PRINTED IN THE UNITED STATES OF AMERICA
DISTRIBUTED BY HYPARXIS PRESS

Book design by Bill Gilbert
based on the original design by Carole Duncan

Cover design by Ronda Gilbert

The former editions of this book were published by
Dionysius Publications

SIXTH EDITION

ISBN 0-9648191-0-4

The cover: The transformations of the mean analogy. See pp. 101-102.

Contents

IS IT ALL RELATIVE?

A Play on Plato's Theatetus

Characters: Harry; Joseph; Elea; Euripides
Scene: The Greek Corner Restaurant

PART ONE

HARRY: Hi, Joe. It's been a while since I saw you last. I'd ask what's new but I've already heard a great deal. So, what is this I hear about the talks that have been going on around here? I can't believe what I've heard. Elea here heard that you got converted. You, of all people! She couldn't, or maybe wouldn't, fill in any of the details. She just said that things like that have been happening. I figured I might as well find out directly from you, so that's why I phoned you to meet us. When you suggested that we meet here I wasn't too sold on it because I hadn't been here before—but darn if it's not a nice place. Elea, by the way, wanted to tag along. Waiter, could we get two more coffees over here? Thanks.

JOSEPH: Nice to see you again. It has been awhile since you've been around here. Now, Elea, what have you stirred up? Unless perhaps you're referring to my interest in Plato, but that's not a conversion, is it?

ELEA: I'm just tagging along, Joseph, as Harry put it so nicely.

HARRY: She didn't say it, I did. We just had a little talk and she got bugged by what I called her, so she's a little bent out of shape. Let's forget about it; it doesn't really matter anyway. So she didn't say converted, I did.
　　Tell me just one thing. How can you—or anyone else for that matter—change so much as to get involved in philosophy? You have never been the sort to fall for a pitch, so I figured something strange must be happening.

JOSEPH: It really must have taken time for the word to get around if you're talking about the talks I think you're referring to.

HARRY: But the way I heard it, I believed it must have been just the other day. You know I've been away for awhile at UCSB and I went to Chicago and thereabouts for a couple of years, but that's over now and I've finished with my degree and with travelling around. We've been through a lot together—in the past that is—haven't we? So, why not level with me? What are you into philosophy for?

JOSEPH: You must have gotten some great insights into philosophy as you traveled about, while those of us here had to be content with exploring ideas among ourselves.

HARRY: If that's an attempt at sarcasm I'll ignore it, but only if you'll fill me in on what I've missed. But you know what? I learned something at SB that you'll never get at your Golden West College—and it's no secret. There is nothing happening in philosophy. Even the best brains in it argue that it would be best to close it all down, throw it out of the colleges and universities and discourage students from getting into it. You know why? I'll tell you! There is really no view better than any other. Even if it seems like there's a better view it's really just a clever argument at work. Everything is a matter of interpretation and everyone interprets to preserve their own bias. It's not that some views won't get you more—for believing 'em or pretending to believe 'em. It's simple. If you want to succeed, believe what's being believed. You know, *when in Rome do as the Romans do*, and that's all there is to it. That's the only advice anyone needs. Take the interpretation that you can do the most with and get the most from; that's all there is to it.

JOSEPH: You want a summary of what's been happening, is that right?

HARRY: Yeah, but make sure you include who started the ball rolling and where it's going and how you got into the act.

JOSEPH: Okay, let's back up for a minute. You see, even though I was present at the earlier talks, my participation didn't start until later. It all started one night when I was having coffee with some of our friends right here at The Greek Corner. One of the owner's friends heard us talking in our usual manner and he said we certainly were having fun joking around, but, since we lacked a certain discipline, it was unlikely that we could ever rise above humor.

We laughed and asked, "What's the need for discipline to say what we feel?" Now, what's interesting is that this was all done in a spirit of fun, but some of us began to wonder just where this discussion was going when he said that unless we learn to explore ideas in a certain way we would never be able to reach understanding—much less understand one another.

HARRY: Wait a minute. You mean you guys were just clowning around and having fun when he came along and said you weren't understanding one another? Now, that's a laugh! You're laughing and joking and he said you weren't understanding one another?

JOSEPH: It got even more interesting when he threw out a challenge. He said that none of us can understand himself, or anyone else, unless we give up or see through what we believe in. And that if we can't do that, it is unlikely that we can reach a deeper understanding of anything else either. Masking his seriousness behind a bit of playfulness he said he would offer a free cup of coffee to anyone who could prove him wrong, but he insisted on one condition.

HARRY: So what was his condition? Who is he? Some Zen nut? A Zorba type that floated into town? Go ahead, what was his condition? I'd like to hear that! And tell me who took him up on it and how did it go?

JOSEPH: The condition was that first we would have to understand his position.

HARRY: You're kidding! No, I guess you're not. Wait a minute. Did he elect himself to judge whether or not you understood him?

Because everyone judges differently. You know what I mean? So who's to say whether or not someone understands something or not? Him? That's absurd since each man perceives differently. You know that!

JOSEPH: I agree that each of us perceives things from our own unique viewpoint, but you don't know it just because you perceive it, or else we would know Chinese or Greek whenever we see it written. Surely you're not saying that perception and knowledge are the same, are you?

HARRY: Of course, and I don't mean merely seeing or perceiving, I mean any experience—whatever a person experiences, exists for them—is and has to be true to the person experiencing it. Now, that's totally obvious, since you are the only one who can say what you experience. Who can say that you don't experience what you say you experience? Surely, you alone know what you experience!

JOSEPH: Because?

HARRY: Why are you playing dumb? Everyone knows that each of us perceives from our own position in life and in our own way. There are no better or superior ways, there are merely different ways. You can try to make this difficult, but it's not. It's obvious that whatever seems true to anyone is true to him to whom it seems so—and that's all there is to it! Who can possibly disprove me when I say I understand you? You? Him?

JOSEPH: But would you now say you have knowledge of it simply because you have seen or encountered it in some way in your experience?

HARRY: Sure, but what're you getting at?

JOSEPH: If each of us has our own truth, each of us should be able to fashion a unique view of life, or philosophy, shouldn't we?

HARRY: Sure, to each his own. As I recall you're the one who was always quipping that philosophy is like belly buttons—everyone has one and no one needs anyone else's. So, why are you into Plato?

JOSEPH: Frankly, once I got inside his dialogues I learned a great deal—much more than I ever expected.

HARRY: Dialogues! His were all staged, none were historical, don't you know that? Everyone has their own view, and you can't change that. Every view becomes an interpretation, and that's all there is.

That's why no one can really know another person, and, what's more, there is no reason to go any further because all you have to do is to look around and you'll see that we do well enough without any need for this thing called knowledge. There are fashions in philosophy like anything else. What's in today is out tomorrow. Surely, you know that what we call knowledge is merely what is accepted by the fashion-setters of the day for this or that purpose. To study someone else's philosophy may be fun for some people, but why get into all that old stuff? It's always better to express your own experience in your own terms than to use someone else's. Why? Because it expresses your experience, not theirs.

JOSEPH: You know, Harry, I once held beliefs similar to yours and would proudly proclaim them to one and all. Recall my old position, how I used to argue that anything is merely the sum of all the ways it could be perceived by anyone?

HARRY: If you don't believe in that anymore, do you believe in Plato? Whatever that would mean! Just how do you plan on explaining it? Lecture us.

JOSEPH: I'll take you through what others have taken me through.

HARRY: I don't get it. What's in it for you? Like playing teacher?

JOSEPH: I am interested in the hold these ideas can have on us and what it takes to break free of them. Simple as that, Harry. So, why don't I put a few questions to you—if you don't mind.

HARRY: You've got to be kidding! I'm not going to get into some cross-examination game just to satisfy your curiosity. I can't really believe you are serious about all this.

    Say, Elea, you got me into this. Why don't you play? Or are you still bugged? I'd rather listen for awhile, but I'm really not into dueling with words.

JOSEPH: Sure, I'd like to talk with Elea, but first I'd like you to know that I'm serious about this matter. You see, I really don't understand what those ideas mean, and what's more, I don't think you understand them either.

HARRY: You've got to be kidding!

JOSEPH: Then let me ask you this, Harry. If what seems true to anyone is true to him to whom it seems so, then would you allow a carpenter to perform brain surgery on you just because it seems to him that he can do it?

HARRY: That's ridiculous, of course not!

JOSEPH: Are we required to go along with someone who believes in such things?

HARRY: Not when you put it that way.

JOSEPH: Well, if you were on a flight to San Francisco, would you do your best to persuade the Captain to allow a fellow passenger, who had been drinking and admitted he couldn't fly an airplane, to attempt to land the airplane simply because it seemed to him that he could do so?

HARRY: Here you go again. Of course not!

JOSEPH: Or is it that we only tolerate the people who hold that position as long as they have no authority to act it out? Don't we tolerate them because we don't want to be rude and say what we really think? But if we were in danger, wouldn't we reject their claim as absurd and quickly look for someone with the knowledge to get us out of danger? It's because of this reasoning that I think no one really believes that this position could possibly be true; and I don't think you're any different from the rest of us.

HARRY: I should've known you'd take it in a way that would turn it inside out. You're making it absurd by treating it as a joke, but that won't change a thing because everybody believes as l do. But not in the way you think. That's for certain. But look here. Who can deny that as long as someone holds something true for themselves that it will continue to be true for them until they change their mind and see something else as true?

JOSEPH: Indeed, that is the way some men hold to their opinions, somewhat like fickle lovers. But would you say those who know geometry, physics, music, and the like, hold to their ideas in a way similar to fickle ones?

HARRY: Well, the point is that you have to agree that people only hold what they believe to be true for a certain period of time. And that, of course, is my point. Nothing is ever proven in the complete and final sense. Changes occur, new theories, new facts, it all changes, so it's only true as long as you believe it.

JOSEPH: But, Harry, aren't the reasons for changing one's opinions the important thing?

HARRY: Yes, and no. The real point is to appear as if you really know what you're talking about. In both cases you've got to make others believe you really know what you're talking about. You have to persuade and convince your beloved that what you say is true, and teachers have to persuade their students that the proofs in geometry are believable and true. Sure, maybe they do it differently, but they both have to convince, don't they?

JOSEPH: Well, it certainly seems to me that the topic has changed, and now we are trying to understand what convinces and justifies accepting one kind of reasoning in geometry and another kind of reasoning among lovers.

HARRY: You don't have to stay on one subject, do you? Why not let your talking take whatever twists and turns it wants? The point is to convince, and whoever does it best wins. Talk among lovers, beloveds, teachers, and students of geometry and whatnot has the same goal. It is always the same; it is, of course, merely to appear as if you know your stuff. So it's all rather simple. Whatever difference there may be among them all doesn't make a difference, my dear friend, because even those who seem to know things, like geometry, only say what's convinced them. And it would still seem to those others—those who don't know those things—that the geometrician, physicist or musician are knowers.

JOSEPH: But don't those who know use a different kind of reasoning than those who don't know?

HARRY: But when you strip it down to the essentials do you believe they are really different? One may last a little longer, but in the end it's the same game of persuasion. All the so-called facts discovered today become tomorrow's folly. How much would you pay for a chemistry book in perfect condition that was published in 1910? And how much will today's best proofs be worth in fifty years? All those smug know-it-all teachers know this, but they still play as if their answers are final and complete.

JOSEPH: Sure enough, but doesn't that mean that knowledge is ever growing and progressing?

HARRY: Yes—and no. Today's best theory lasts how long? Who is to say it is better? You? They just get more of the same; it's not any better just more of it.

JOSEPH: Let me ask you to consider this one thing. Of those who you say are knowers of geometry, do they offer demonstrations and a variety of proofs to support their claim, or do they merely appear as if they know?

HARRY: No, they appear to have proofs.

JOSEPH: And surely we won't be mislead or fooled by their conclusions if the demonstrations and proofs are sound, will we?

HARRY: No, not if they really are sound, but you never know if they will really last. How can you be sure that some insight into math, physics, or whatnot, might not overthrow all those earlier proofs or even the very idea of what a proof is?

JOSEPH: Harry, a proof is a proof, or it wouldn't be a proof.

HARRY: You know what? You're a believer, a believer in proofs, and that makes you no different than the rest of us. *Knowing* is a myth. You can't really prove anything.

JOSEPH: If something is proven it proves there is a proof or it couldn't prove it.

HARRY: No way! Proofs aren't all the same, don't you know that? There are a whole bunch of them; some they call elegant and some sloppy.

JOSEPH: A sloppy proof?

HARRY: Sure, you know the one from Geometry where they try to prove two triangles are equal? No, I don't mean equal, I mean congruent—that's the word for it.

JOSEPH: Well, they do it, don't they?

HARRY: The so-called *proof* is phoney. They pick one of them and land it on the other and claim they fit nicely without any overlapping. You call *that* a proof? Is *that* reasoning? All they do is drop something on top of something else and holler, "See, they are equal. They fit." So much for your proofs. So, dear old buddy, unless you prove a proof proves a proof, I'll just call you a believer. I heard a professor argue there are no flawless proofs, or do you know one that is so perfect that no one can doubt its truth? Come on Joseph, do you have one? But you don't, and neither does anyone else.

JOSEPH: Well, that's something I'll have to consider. Let's go back to what you just mentioned. Could those who have no knowledge of Geometry know whether or not a geometrician knows geometry or appears to know it if they know nothing of Geometry themselves?

HARRY: There's no mystery about it; you can always tell who knows Geometry or anything else by the way they talk. Even if you know very little about geometry yourself, after being in a new class for just a few minutes you can tell whether a professor gives that appearance of knowing his stuff or not.

JOSEPH: Of course, you're right, Harry, but only to some degree. For surely you're not saying that you know sufficiently about a subject to judge whether or not your professor knows, are you? If you knew either as much as or more than he knows, then why would you be taking a course from him? Don't you mean you can judge whether or not a professor appears to you to be confident and secure enough to get up before a class full of students and teach them?

HARRY: And to know how to judge that appearance is to know, isn't it? Sure it is!

JOSEPH: In any case, wouldn't you say that we have been fooled by those who give the appearance of being knowers but who know far less than the way they appear?

HARRY: Yes, that's so. They're the ones that merely bluff. I don't mean them.

JOSEPH: Then are you thinking about those who fool others by giving the appearance of being knowers but are only familiar with well rehearsed parts of their subject?

HARRY: No, I don't mean them; I know that type too. They pull rank and list their credentials, as if degrees and academic appointments make a difference. They'll turn you into their enemy, but for what? To preserve their mask. You know what? That knowing game makes enemies, divides friends, and behind it all is just a game of power. All this for nothing. There's no reason to take differences as seriously as that. Each of us is right in our own way; each of us is as good as the next man. We should just allow differences since they don't really matter anyway.

JOSEPH: But if differences don't make any difference, Harry, why would those who want to appear as knowers go through all the trouble of giving such a good appearance? Now, doesn't that mean that they really do appreciate the difference since they try so hard to imitate those they try to be like?

HARRY: No. Don't you see that they eradicate the difference? When they have truly mastered the appearance they will be seen as knowers. Don't forget that's what knowing is all about. It's not to be a knower—whatever that is—but to appear as knowing. And who is to say that is not knowing? Anyway, if you can get someone who can act like a President elected into office, then you don't just have an actor for a President, you have a President, right? There you have it. That's the perfect case. There is no difference when the appearance becomes the actual.

JOSEPH: That reminds me of a story–

HARRY: Spare me your stories. I'm not interested in those clever tales you're supposed to puzzle over. I just heard one from Elea when we were coming over here, and, frankly, I didn't see anything to it.

ELEA: I asked Harry for his answer to a question I've heard you ask—only it pushed him out of shape. Every once and awhile it comes back to me and I kind of chuckle over it. It's the one that asks if the woman was right to become furious at her lover when she discovered the reason he could appear so ideal—even anticipating and meeting her every wish and desire—was because he had secretly made a copy of her personal diary and modeled himself to fit her dream wish.

HARRY: I just said that it shouldn't have made any difference to her since he gave her what she wanted. That's why you read menus, so you don't have to guess what can be served. So no more of those pointless stories. Just stay on the point.

JOSEPH: You are right, Harry, we should stay on the point. Well, let me go back to our last point and ask this. When you can't distinguish between the real and the appearance—or determine the difference between the knowers and those who act the part of knowers—do you still want to call that kind of thing knowing?

HARRY: Maybe so, maybe not. It's really simple. Men strut on the stage of life like peacocks acting out the game of knowing, as someone once said.

JOSEPH: But, Harry, if we realized we were fooled, then we had to recognize they gave a good appearance of being knowers. Doesn't that mean that at one time we couldn't distinguish reality from its appearance but at another time we could?

HARRY: Yeah, that's true, I guess. We can be fooled by a good performance or even a good appearance.

JOSEPH: Now if I, or someone else, asked you to name that reality behind the appearance, you would likely answer, wouldn't you? What would you have to say?

HARRY: Knowledge! Is that the answer you want?

JOSEPH: And isn't it fair to say that whether you are being fooled or not you were only judging an appearance, instead of the presence or absence of knowledge? Now, Harry, can you judge whether the given appearance is actually an appearance if you have no knowledge of the reality behind it?

HARRY: Go ahead and conclude from your little word games, but I don't believe you have to conclude that way. All is belief; there's nothing other than belief.

JOSEPH: But how can we escape the conclusion? Aren't you very knowledgeable? Just recall what you have said. Don't you claim to know that all who have mastered any part of science, math, and other subjects can only give an appearance of having knowledge but do not have knowledge? You know, too, that the facts of today are tomorrow's folly, don't you? You know that the best appearance of knowing is indistinguishable from knowledge as long as it is believed to be true, and so it must be knowledge, mustn't it? Aren't these some of the things you say you know?

HARRY: I'll tell you something. It's true that I may have overstated my case for a moment, but my position is still sound. It may or may not apply to math and science, but it does especially apply to matters of morals, ethics, politics and religion! For in each of these areas it is easy to see that no one is wiser than another. And since all judgments are relative to one's culture, then no one can say one is superior to another.

JOSEPH: Well, it is good to finally get your position on its firmest ground.

HARRY: Sure, sure. You're one of those people who try to nail down what can't be hammered down. Now, go ahead and ask me whatever you wish.

JOSEPH: When people become members of this or that political or religious group, what would you say they are trying to achieve? Or do you believe people come together and form groups for no reason?

HARRY: To get what they can't achieve alone.

JOSEPH: Some benefit?

HARRY: What else?

JOSEPH: Then, wouldn't you say there are likely to be times when the leaders of these groups make decisions which they hope will benefit their members?

HARRY: Sure enough, and they are likely make decisions to benefit themselves, too.

JOSEPH: And do you think it would be likely for each member of the group to reach totally different conclusions from those of their leaders regarding what may benefit or harm their particular group—since, according to you, each person views things from a different and unique position?

HARRY: No, I don't believe each person would necessarily have a different opinion—but they might.

JOSEPH: And isn't it also likely that the groups' leaders may consult with others and discuss the issues facing them?

HARRY: Yes.

JOSEPH: And wouldn't we call those with whom they consult advisors? For even those who only listen to their own advice can be said to have an advisor—themselves.

HARRY: Of course.

JOSEPH: But if advice is offered, does that mean it will be true just because it seems to be? What do you think? Will it necessarily be true just because it seems so?

HARRY: Why wouldn't it be true to them?

JOSEPH: Consider this. If what seems true is in reality true, then, in that case, no man or institution could ever make a mistake.

HARRY: You take everything too literally, Joseph.

JOSEPH: But don't you think that some people are better in advising than others so that some advice is better than other advice? Or, Harry, perhaps you know leaders who prefer to discuss such issues with those in their group who are least able to discuss them intelligently.

HARRY: You made your point.

JOSEPH: Then you agree that the art of governing depends on being able to distinguish the good advice from the bad?

HARRY: Yes.

JOSEPH: And poor advice is poor when it mistakes what is taken to be advantageous?

HARRY: Maybe you can say that.

JOSEPH: You mean you wouldn't say that some groups do better and so are better when they have benefited from good advice as to what is advantageous to them?

HARRY: Logically that may follow, that's all.

JOSEPH: And wouldn't you say that if the advice fails, isn't it because it wasn't able to determine what would be advantageous or
harmful?

HARRY: I guess I agree.

JOSEPH: And isn't such advice concerned with the future, because
it surely isn't something that is visible which we can perceive or
experience before us; for the future is not yet but that which is yet
to come to pass?   But didn't you say that *knowledge was percep-*
tion?   And that's something that must take place in the present,
right?

HARRY: Yeah, that's so.

JOSEPH: So that while each group may have different goals they
all use the same way to judge how one view is better or wiser than
another, do they not?

HARRY: So?

JOSEPH: So? Well, don't groups benefit when the advice turns
out to their advantage? Surely, when the advice allows some excellence to develop doesn't the group function better through that
better advice?

HARRY: Only if they believe it to be so.

JOSEPH: Don't you think that some groups survive because they
have acted upon the kind of advice that allowed them to survive
rather than perish?   Isn't that better advice?

HARRY: Survival? They survived because they believed in the advice and acted upon it, that's all.

JOSEPH: And does that have to do with what was going on around
them?

HARRY: You know what they say, don't you?   It's the power of
positive thinking that makes things happen.   Maybe not always,
but there are enough of us who see it.

JOSEPH: Well, would you still say that whatever anyone believes will come to pass—must come to pass—simply because at some moment it seems true to him to whom it seems true?

HARRY: Well—maybe.

JOSEPH: Then, consider another thing, Harry. If it were important for you to determine whether the information or advice you received were sound, wouldn't you want to discover the truth of the matter for yourself?

HARRY: Maybe, but in the end we can only accept what we can believe, right?

JOSEPH: Would you say that if you believed in something strongly that believing would make it so? Indeed, there are some men and institutions who seem to be shielded from criticism even though they continue advising us and warning us about their belief of an impending inevitable catastrophe, and then, rather than abandon the belief when the event fails to occur, they still insist it will occur sometime in the near future. Now, it certainly seemed true to them that it was, or will be, inevitable. They can't give up the belief, for every moment and circumstance they believe it will be true, yet it never has been true. So, in what sense is your position like theirs?

HARRY: I'm not sure where this is going. Say, Joseph, why don't you include Elea in this talk?

ELEA: Just when I was getting to enjoy this, you pull out. I'll tell you what I do think, Joseph. There still might be something in what Harry says though not as much as he believes. But I came along to hear how you'd answer Harry's charges, and now it looks like I'm about to be pulled in.

HARRY: Hey, yeah! Joseph, what's going on? You've turned the tables around. You were going to tell us what has been happening around here and now look at this—you have us defending our views while you get off the hook!

JOSEPH: Perhaps, but remember the Greek's challenge—that we can't understand unless we see through a belief and give up the one that blocks us from understanding. Well, Harry, what belief do you think it is?

HARRY: You've got to be kidding.

JOSEPH: Yes, this belief of yours is the same belief that dominates not only your mind but many others as well. It's this belief we are discussing that keeps us from appreciating and utilizing the furthermost reach of the intellect.

HARRY: I don't know if I am going to like this or not. You may think I'm defending some position, but I don't believe so. I just hold that there are no real positions in philosophy—only naive commitments to absurdities. You might be able to argue better than I do, but that won't mean a damn thing because I'll walk away believing what I've always believed and so will you.

ELEA: Let me ask you something, Harry, if you don't mind a question or two.

HARRY: Ask, my dear, ask anything at all.

ELEA: Harry, isn't believing in Christianity, or any religion, believing that one view is better than another? More than that, isn't believing in something admitting that it is better to have something to believe in than nothing?

HARRY: What? Whose side are you on? I thought you were only interested in going along with me.

ELEA: I just thought of something, Harry. You care enough to strongly oppose Joseph's position. You get upset when your view that all is relative is challenged. Now, how can you reconcile that with your position? How can you be bugged? It is all relative, isn't it?

HARRY: Yes, it sure as hell is. So, I'm relatively bugged about my relative position. So what? It's your turn to get bugged, or to shut up.

ELEA: No—You stay in as long as you can, and I'll come in when I want. It's not as easy as you thought it would be, is it?

HARRY: Well, I'm okay right now—so let's get on with it.

JOSEPH: Then, let us return to the other point you raised, Harry. It is equally interesting, and it's likely to be related in some way to what we have done. Let me raise the issue in another context— just for some fun—and it may provide a way to understand it. You say my position must be wrong since so many of your teachers and other authorities oppose it. And that some of them even go so far as to argue that to disagree with their position is, in itself, a mark that one is naive and unfit for mature intellectual reflection. Am I reflecting your position accurately?

HARRY: Yes.

JOSEPH: Well, suppose I was teaching a class in philosophy and were to advance the idea that, in mathematics, A times B does not always equal B times A and that 2 times 3 is not always 3 times 2.

HARRY: Someone in the math department would have a good laugh at your expense. That's for damn sure.

JOSEPH: And in a similar way, suppose I were to advance the notion that the idea of experimentation in the sciences is folly and should be regarded as being merely window dressing to confound fools.

HARRY: The same would go for those in the science labs.

JOSEPH: But apart from their having a laugh, is it not likely that they could present me with some reasoned explanations, demonstrations, and proofs that would challenge and, possibly, cause me to reject the laughable view I was holding in class?

HARRY: Sure, I see what you want. You want equal time to show them that this idea, that all positions are subjective and relative, is wrong. But you, of all people, ought to know they have as much right as anyone to give their personal views on these issues. Are you going for censorship, Joseph?

JOSEPH: No, of course not. What I'm talking about are those views which are often dropped into the lecture or conversation while talking about other things yet uttered as if they were obvious and beyond question, very much as any prejudice might be inserted in discussions. Indeed, when given a chance to address an audience there aren't many people who can resist the chance to interject their own personal views into their talk. For we both know that there are times when teachers will play philosopher in front of their classes and are seldom, if ever, challenged on the shallowness of their views, including this very relativity position. And I am not just talking about your professors, am I?

HARRY: Now I know where you are going with all this. You believe that the idea that all is relative can be argued against. That's okay—that's your belief. But look, Joe, quite frankly, I don't know what I'd believe if you were right and that was true. It just can't be true. It's just too weird to believe that all those who insisted that there's nothing going on in philosophy could be wrong. Like— why would they say that? Do you know what I mean?

JOSEPH: Elea, would you care to explore these ideas? For I think our friend Harry might prefer to observe for the time being. Is that right?

HARRY: Actually, I would like to see Elea take her turn with you. I'm beginning to believe she knows more about this than she admitted.

JOSEPH: Well, Elea, do you want to inherit this discussion?

ELEA: Yes, and no.

JOSEPH: Explain, please.

ELEA: Well, I'm not sure that I have this belief, but I am beginning to think that one I have might be connected with it in some way. This may sound kind of strange, but I like to hear these kinds of talks because I'm kind of burned out on what passes for entertainment. No, I don't mean it that way. What I think can't really be separated from my being me. Do you understand? Look at it this way—when I hear discussions I begin thinking that someone has the answer somewhere. It's got to have been researched by someone. Isn't there a book on it? So everything is relative to this or that expert's opinion, and those opinions are not very interesting anyway. That's what I think.

JOSEPH: A lot of what passes for knowledge is boring.

ELEA: I can go along with Harry's views but not because I personally hold them. Let's just say I've heard them all my life and I've never heard anyone silence them, at least not to my satisfaction.

JOSEPH: And is that what you'd like to do? Silence them?

ELEA: I used to get into some discussions that were going along fine when some fool would throw out one of those aphorisms, which is what I call them, and that either ends the discussion as everyone retreats into a silent stupor, or I end up feeling foolish for not being able to silence the fool. "What seems true to anyone is true to him to whom it seems so," was also my father's favorite aphorism, and he'd put an end to any discussion with it. And if that didn't work he'd say, "Anyway, all good questions can only be answered by experts," and he would add, "And you aren't one!" Sure, I can represent those views, but if I get into any trouble I'm sure going to ask for help.

But, Joseph, before we begin could you order something for me to go along with the coffee?

JOSEPH: You know, that's a good idea! There's Euripides. Euripides, some Baklava, please, and keep the coffee coming. Thanks.

Say, Elea I'd like you to know that I can understand your position because I grew up with those too. And even so, I've seen you sitting in on a few of the talks. So, I would like to ask you, Elea, about those aphorisms that you referred to, but first, I would like to know something more about why you are drawn to talks like these.

ELEA: I'd really like to think that something matters. I think I listen for it but don't trust what I hear because so much of what is usually talked about ends up being nothing other than comparing opinions about something that some expert has some answer to, or worse yet, some reason for *not* asking about it. Maybe I can put it another way—what good is discussing anything if nothing I ever hear matters to me personally? Like, I don't have a stake in any system or political matter except, maybe, in stopping them from turning the earth into a cesspool.

JOSEPH: Well, we do share some things. I wonder if the biggest task in saving ourselves and our planet may not be to see through the beliefs that prevent us from saving ourselves. And whether we would see anyone saying that everything is relative as we all sink deeper into that cesspool. So now I'd like to hear those deadly aphorisms you just mentioned.

ELEA: Sure, that's easy. I hear them all the time. When you string them all together you've got the wisdom of the ages: *It's all relative. Who's to say who is right or wrong? Every culture has its own rights and wrongs. Don't make value judgements. To each his own.* And the cutest of them all: *What's true to anyone is true to him to whom it seems so.* It all boils down to *it doesn't matter.* But here I am, still looking for something that matters. I can come up with others if you give me a little time.

JOSEPH: No, Elea, it looks like you have enough of them. You've been observing from the side lines, and I'm glad to see you've crossed over. It's good to explore these notions with someone like yourself; it is a way of testing our understanding. Another thing, if it should turn out that I need help I might be able to call on Sophronicus—he's the friend of the owner I mentioned—and discuss it with him and his circle of friends. However, that's not likely to help me now since he usually comes around later in the day. So, let's explore it together.

ELEA: With a name like that, I think I'm in for a surprise. It's clear you've explored these ideas before and probably many times, but what do you see when you test someone's understanding?

JOSEPH: That may not be easy to explain, but I'll try. Whenever
it's possible to examine these ideas in dialogues I find it reward-
ing because it gives me a chance to view them through someone
else's understanding.

ELEA: That doesn't answer my question, does it?

JOSEPH: Well, what I find remarkable by going through dialogues
like this one is that I can focus on what, to me, is mysterious:
making beliefs visible, understanding what maintains them, and
what brings about their dissolution. You see, these ideas seem to
possess such vast power over men's minds, yet once they are seen
for what they are, they dissipate like the morning mist. But if
there is one I can't resolve, then I always discover that there is
something I overlooked in that very belief, perhaps in the way it is
put or the manner it is being held. Now, to the extent that I was
unaware of it, I, too, held that belief. When this happens, I am
interested in discovering why I held to it and why it escaped my
notice.

ELEA: I can't say you aren't optimistic. Equally, I can't say your
answer was good enough for me either—but I don't know what
else to say. Anyway, I'll try to do my best, and either way it seems
I can't lose.

JOSEPH: Now that we're going to explore this position, we must
come to an understanding of just what are its parts and what binds
those parts together into a whole. After that it should be an easy
task to name it and make sure that its name fits. But what its
proper name should be, I think, will require some time for reflection. However, since that task may take awhile, it looks like we
are going to have to keep referring to it as this position for now.
       First then, what is this position? And when someone holds it
to be true, do they want their words to be treated seriously, or do
they advance this position merely for dramatic purposes and humor, without really having any position themselves? Does their
position both challenge and question the legitimacy of other systems of thought while boasting that it asserts no position of its

own? Can the proponents of this position criticize others and yet escape scrutiny themselves?

ELEA: Well, if they're joking they do so very seriously—in deadly earnest. They always want their words to be taken as a challenge; you might say that the way they challenge others is like the way some men show their contempt for those who disagree with them. I'd say they are often rude, especially to those who dare suggest there may be some truth.

JOSEPH: Surely they challenge others, but don't they also claim that what they say is true? Aren't they saying that whatever seems true to anyone is true to him to whom it seems so? And don't they regard that statement to be true for everyone?

ELEA: They sure do!

JOSEPH: But consider this. If I make a judgment that my sandals are good for my feet, who would be the best judge of whether or not my statement is true? Should it be someone who has knowledge of how shoes and sandals affect the feet, or someone who knows nothing of this?

ELEA: Someone who has that knowledge.

JOSEPH: And if it were important for you to know whether or not my statement was true, wouldn't you want to discover on what basis I made my judgment?

ELEA: Of course.

JOSEPH: So, in general, if someone were to ask another on what basis they claim their judgments are true, wouldn't they be pleased to share with them what had convinced them that what they say is true?

ELEA: Yes.

JOSEPH: And do you agree that whatever has convinced them must be different from what is said to be true?

ELEA: Of course.

JOSEPH: And when asked what convinced them of this position
           that "what seems true to anyone is true to him to whom it seems
           so," what other answer can they give than "if it seems so it must be
           so"?

ELEA: I think none other.

JOSEPH: And in a similar way, if you were asked, "What is it again
           that you say is true?" would you give, "What seems true to anyone
           is true to him to whom it seems so"?

ELEA: Well, if I gave you that, it would seem to me that they
           aren't different, at least, the idea of *seems so* appears to me to be
           central to both. Harry, what do you think about this, are they the
           same or different?

HARRY: That happens to be a compound sentence containing both.
           But just because it's got two parts in one doesn't mean those parts
           are the same.

ELEA: And what of those two parts?

HARRY: Look here, if you feel you're right and base your judg-
           ment on that fact, then that's the way it seems to you, and the
           judgment is based upon the way it appears to you. Now do you
           understand, Elea? Don't fall for his rhetorical arguments; just stay
           in there and stick to the position because there's nothing weak
           about the position itself.

ELEA: It just goes round and round.

JOSEPH: This question about the parts is a good one, but I have
           another problem with the meaning of the term *appears*. Now,
           should I address this to you, Elea, or to Harry?

HARRY: Elea!

JOSEPH: Then in terms of this position, when they say what ap-
           pears to them, do they mean what they perceive?

ELEA: Yes.

JOSEPH: Because they're fond of announcing that each man perceives differently and that no one has any special or privileged viewpoint that might give them a superior view of things, so they conclude that there can only be different views of things. Now then, if I were to ask you what convinced them that their statement is true, I imagine you'd have a ready answer.

ELEA: Yes. They'd say that what appears to them is true and can be derived from the fact that knowledge is nothing other than perception.

JOSEPH: And if something is true, Elea, don't you agree we should be able to apply it and test it in various situations?

ELEA: Since their position applies to what they think is true for man's experience, it would have to be tested and proven in our everyday experiences.

JOSEPH: Now, suppose we were to ask a believer of this position whether or not they can know something they do not know. Consider, do you believe someone who knew nothing of ancient Greek could read it simply because he could perceive the pages of an ancient Greek manuscript?

ELEA: No, of course not.

JOSEPH: But according to their theory, if they perceive it, they should know it. But what is it they would know? Certainly not what they don't know. Do you think we're taking their position too literally?

ELEA: Perhaps. I'm not sure.

JOSEPH: And if all it took to know another person would be to perceive that person, wouldn't we all be knowledgeable about one another? And wouldn't it follow that each one of us would be a very profound psychologist?

ELEA: Oh, I see how this can be fun!

JOSEPH: Then according to what we have said, what would you
say about those of us who are nearsighted or farsighted?

ELEA: Good. Why, the nearsighted would only know things
close up and the farsighted would only know things far away, and
neither would know anything in between!

JOSEPH: Now you make one up.

ELEA: Here's one: when lovers turn the lights off they'd become
ignorant of their beloveds, and they wouldn't know how to relate
to their beloveds or to themselves.

JOSEPH: Yes, merely by taking their words seriously—literally—
we can have a lot of fun with this position. Wouldn't they have to
agree that in the evening hours men become dimwits and, finally,
they become ignorant when the dark of night closes in? Here's
another one we can chuckle over: if they mean that what they perceive is the way it truly is, then we can point out to them the curious fact that men appear or disappear simply by moving towards
us or away from us.

ELEA: The other day I was down at the beach at sunset and saw
the sun disappear into the ocean. The sun must have gotten wet.

JOSEPH: If knowledge is perception and you see the sun move in
the heavens, then it surely must be happening just the way you see
it. Yes! The geocentric theory must be true.
      Try a new approach, Elea. Can you see it, experience it, and
then remember it, but fail to know it?

ELEA: No, of course not.

JOSEPH: But according to their position, when you are remember-
ing something and not seeing it, can you claim to know that thing?

ELEA: I guess not. In fact, if you once turn your head around
and are no longer seeing what was in front of your face, you will
become ignorant of what you were just experiencing.

JOSEPH: That's right, Elea.

ELEA: I just remembered something! You are still perceiving it when you remember it! I am seeing an image of what I once saw, so I am perceiving it, am I not? That is a kind of perceiving, isn't it?

JOSEPH: Whether it is really a kind of knowledge is our question, Elea. When you recall how the sun appeared to descend into the ocean, would you say that's the way it is or the way it appeared?

ELEA: Like before, only an appearance, not knowledge.

JOSEPH: So if knowledge is the way things seem then it is only an appearance of knowledge, not knowledge.

ELEA: Right. Now what else can we do to it? It sure has a fun side to it.

JOSEPH: Consider this alternative. If we both see something and share the same viewpoint, would we have the same knowledge?

ELEA: Yes.

JOSEPH: Then seeing—as seeing—results in the same thing? And as seeing, it would be the same knowledge?

ELEA: Sure, the knowledge would be the same.

JOSEPH: Then whatever was perceiving would have the same knowledge?

ELEA: In the precise way in which you're speaking—yes.

JOSEPH: Then, if a dog or a cat were perceiving, and if a goat and a pig were perceiving, and if a man and a new born baby were perceiving, wouldn't they all have the same knowledge?

ELEA: It sure goes to the absurd quickly. Do you believe you can still save this theory of yours, Harry?

HARRY: Have you guys finished having your fun yet? Well, I'll tell you something. Joseph, when you get Elea here to agree with you about my position, I'll tell you something, it's not me that's agreeing—it's her! So the pig and the cat have knowledge, and as far as I know they may have the same knowledge as both of you. I'll tell you another thing. You haven't understood the simplest of things: there is no knowledge! And I'll tell you why—because everything is in a state of change, everything is in a state of flux, and that goes for us also. We're never the same. All we can do is catch a glimpse of what changes, and that's why what *seems* true *is* true to him to whom it *seems* so.

JOSEPH: But, Harry, do you really believe everyone is as wise as you?

HARRY: Sure some are wiser! What's wiser? If you can change another person's beliefs to something more flexible than what they've got, then you're the wise one, and by *that* you make another wiser. It's just what I told you! The only advice anyone needs is *when in Rome do as the Romans do*—don't fight 'em, join 'em. Don't laugh, because the wise ones agree with me and the wiser still are those who act on it. Now, Joseph, if it pleases you, then do it. That's all you need to know.

JOSEPH: Do you mean if something pleases you that you can judge it as true? And do you mean anything other than the experience of pleasure when you say it pleases? So, if it pleases and is pleasurable it is therefore true? Do I understand you?

HARRY: Go ahead and have your fun. It's still true.

JOSEPH: But don't we all know from experience that something is higher than pleasure? If eating sugar is pleasurable, is that all you would eat? If laughing pleases you, is that all you would do?

HARRY: Sometimes I feel that you just find reasons to reject whatever I say is true. It really gets trying! Why don't you stop making my position into a joke? I don't care if you find it funny or not. Aren't theories supposed to be capable of being disproved if they are wrong? Okay, then do it if you can—but you can't. All you can do is play the clown and get Elea to join in with you and become a clown herself. In the immortal words of another Harry, *make my day!*

Go ahead and continue with Elea, only, please deal with the issue. You call yourself a philosopher, so let me see you act out your game. That is, if there's anything to it.

JOSEPH: Yes, I'm interested in continuing this discussion with Elea, but, Harry, I'm not doubting your ability, or that of your teachers, to change peoples' beliefs. And I'm not joking about that. It often seems to me that persuading someone to drop one belief for another is very difficult. I think it might be easier to exchange one belief for another than to leave the comfort of belief and seek the kind of understanding that is not based upon fiction.

HARRY: Would you clue me into what that would be? Every system is a fiction, you ought to know that!

JOSEPH: Beyond fiction? That's not easy. I'm not sure of all that, but let me try. I'd say when you move beyond systems of belief into those of understanding and then on to knowledge, you have to face their similarities and differences. The different realms of belief, understanding, knowledge, and wisdom have their structural similarities. It's comprehending their differences that constitutes the corresponding challenges and difficulties. What I mean is, as these differences generate parallel questions, in a similar way, these realms require a different kind of participation.

HARRY: I asked and look what I got! Joseph quotes from his classroom notes. You recite your professors' notes and make believe it makes sense. Didn't you say you were going on to explore something with Elea?

JOSEPH: Well, what do you know? I think you may have caught me there, Harry. And I do believe I was going on a digression. Elea, what do you think? Can we try to test this position together?

ELEA: If it's up to me—go ahead. I'll gladly follow if you lead.

JOSEPH: Good, let's take up Harry's challenge. Elea, could someone claim that they believe something to be true for all mankind and yet not believe that it applies to themselves?

ELEA: That would be contradictory—and rather strange.

JOSEPH: And what is contradictory could hardly be true, could it?

ELEA: No.

JOSEPH: Well, this position that Harry believes to be true for all mankind is one he doesn't believe is true for himself, personally.

ELEA: Really?

JOSEPH: Should the person who holds that each man is a competent judge of the truth of whatever seems true to him be able to judge the truth of Harry's position, or would you say, "No, that's the one thing that he can't judge the truth of"?

ELEA: According to the position, since he can judge all things, he would have to be a competent judge even of the truth of Harry's position.

JOSEPH: And in judging, could he either agree with that position and regard it as true, or disagree with it and regard it as false?

ELEA: Of course. That's what judging is all about.

JOSEPH: Now, about Harry. Doesn't his position claim that he can judge the truth of all things? For suppose we were to find that there was just one thing that Harry couldn't judge the truth of?

ELEA: Well, in that case, since his position claims that he can judge all things, I suppose you would say that at that point he is abandoning his position.

JOSEPH: And according to his position, then, is it possible for someone to either accept or reject his position?

ELEA: Of course.

JOSEPH: For the sake of the argument, would you be willing to hold his position as one you believe to be true?

ELEA: Certainly.

JOSEPH: Then in terms of the position, could you reject it as false if it seemed to you to be so?

ELEA: Sure, that would follow.

JOSEPH: And again, according to his view, could Harry either agree or disagree with your judgment—especially if your judgment was that his position was false?

ELEA: Sure. Wait a minute! He couldn't agree with my judgment or he would be agreeing that his position was false!

JOSEPH: And what would follow if he rejected your judgment that his position was false?

ELEA: Well, for one thing, he would be saying that I can't judge his position as false. Oh! He'd be saying that there is one thing that I can't judge—his position! But that would deny the truth of his own position since he said anyone can judge all things in terms of the way they seem to them!

JOSEPH: Then it appears that if anyone agrees with him that his position is true, then he can judge their judgment as true, but if anyone dares to disagree with him and says his position is false, can he judge that?

ELEA: He can only judge it as an opinion, that's clear, but he can't deal with the implications of judging it true.

JOSEPH: What can he judge? Isn't it true that the only thing he can judge is what seems so?

ELEA: True

JOSEPH: But not whether something is or is not true or false?

ELEA: Right!

JOSEPH: So he can neither say that he can judge all things, nor can he believe another's judgment when they reject his position, even though that's the way it may seem to them. Therefore, he cannot believe his own position.

ELEA: So he ends up like the man who judges that only the men who agree with him are wise. That's very interesting.

JOSEPH: But, Elea, can it really be a theory?

ELEA: Why do you ask?

JOSEPH: Because theories must be capable of being surpassed by newer theories. If not, it's not a theory. Simply put, a theory should be, in principle, capable of being disproved. But Harry's position can't be disproven—so it can't be rejected or surpassed by others.

ELEA: Clever! Therefore, we can conclude it's not a theory. It can never be proven true either! So what is it?

JOSEPH: A personal view or a position of some sort, that's all.

ELEA: And what kind of a viewpoint?

JOSEPH: What do you call something that is asserted as true but cannot be either proven or disproven, something believed in and insisted upon even after its inadequacies become visible, and yet it cannot be rejected?

ELEA: A prejudice!

HARRY: You call it a prejudice? Just look at that so-called argument of Joseph's and you'll find prejudice! How can you go along with that?

ELEA: But it seems right, doesn't it? What's wrong with it?

HARRY: Well, it's not any good, can't you see that?

ELEA: What's wrong with it?

HARRY: Well, for one thing, I'd like to go over it once more. Logical arguments are deceptive, as you ought to know.

ELEA: Would you like to go over it again? Carefully, step by step?

HARRY: Sometime, yes.

ELEA: But you wouldn't be judging it the way it seems, then, would you?

HARRY: Oh! Aren't you the clever one?! Are you getting what you came for, dear Elea?

EURIPIDES: Coffee anyone?

ELEA: You have a good sense of timing, Euripides.

HARRY: Don't believe it. He's been listening in on the whole thing and just waited for a conclusion so he could pour the coffee. Right? And just what do you get out of our little discussion?

EURIPIDES: I hear a lot of talk around here, and you can tell that most of it is empty talk. So when there is real talk you can spot it right away. So when you have some time I'd like to hear what you have been discussing tonight. And my brother, Dimitri, would want to be counted in, too.

ELEA: Do you mean me?

EURIPIDES: I'd be pleased to hear your recollection, or even that of one of your friends here, maybe sometime later.

[INTERLUDE]

PART TWO

HARRY: Your clever way of approaching this issue doesn't carry any weight because most people believe as I do. They couldn't all be wrong and you right. You have to accept the theory of relativity, don't you? Well, everything's relative and that's that! In every culture and in every period of history people have defined things their own way. Everyone interprets everything. I can recall all kinds of teachers, professors and so forth—and they all agree on this one thing. The most accepted theory is nothing other than this: *whatever is believed to be true is true as long as it is supported by believers.* And what is believed? Merely another interpretation. So who are you to think you are right over all of them?

JOSEPH: You certainly came out swinging on that one, Harry, and while there is something in what you say I think is true, there are other parts I'm not sure of.

HARRY: Really? What?

JOSEPH: I'm not sure about all this business of interpreting. When you, or anyone else, reads or hears something do you always interpret it? I mean, if you know what the words mean, do you still find yourself interpreting them?

HARRY: Of course.

JOSEPH: All of it, or only some parts of it?

HARRY: What else? All of it.

JOSEPH: But if you change all of it, how can you say you are reading it? Isn't there something there that remains what it is and you just add something to it?

HARRY: Certainly you don't change it all—wait a minute—just what are you driving at?

JOSEPH: I am wondering about the condition of the material before you interpret it. Is it faulty and you have to save it with your
interpretation? Surely, if it were perfect just as it is you wouldn't
need to interpret it, or would you?

HARRY: It's very simple, nothing to wonder about. As things
change and progress happens, we evolve, so the way you formerly
saw things changes and you gain a new perspective. The old goes
and the new stays; you either throw out the older parts of your
culture and traditions that don't fit with what you know or you
save them with a new interpretation. That's the way you keep your
traditions alive. And when you add to it the new stuff you've discovered, you keep a synthesis between the old and new. That's the
main point of philosophy. Everyone does it for the same reason. I
could add a noble list of philosophers that play this game. I've
studied them at UCSB and they go from Friedrich, Ast, Dilthey,
Schleiermacher, to Heidegger. Come to think of it, I haven't really
thought of them for sometime—actually, this is the first time I've
ever had cause to use them.

JOSEPH: Thanks, that is very helpful, but would it be fair for me
to conclude that they add to or supplement some original work?
And, at the same time, must they not ignore or drop other parts out
of their interpretation?

HARRY: That's a little simplistic but I guess it boils down to that.

JOSEPH: Then, in that way does it gain a significance it didn't
have before? Or is it that it wasn't seen before and they bring it to
light?

HARRY: You could say they do both.

JOSEPH: What is the reason for all this adding and subtracting to
the work? What do you think is the reason for this process going
on and on? Certainly, at some point, with all the changes, it becomes a new work, doesn't it?

HARRY: Well, the old stuff could be outdated, in error, or for some
reason objectionable, so it is interpreted. The name of the game is

hermeneutics. Look here, don't you grasp the point that religion and history fill a gap in our lives? No, it's not just a gap, it's more than that because they cover a mystery and that mystery happens to be us. Interpreting helps make it possible to look at the past and face the future. Maybe you can take looking at the past, but for me it's blood soaked, every single damn era has its own madness. Hegel said it right when he said that the blank pages of history are the periods of human happiness because that was when nothing really was happening in history. You like sloshing through the corruption of even the best periods of time, go ahead and find the Kennedys' Achilles heel, dredge up the muck on Reagan, or the sins of the Popes and such stuff, but most of us don't object when someone glorifies the past.

JOSEPH: So now the truth is out! History puts the smile on the monstrous record of man's deeds. Come on, Harry, what's more absurd than that? Philosophy or history? Do you know what you like? Cosmetics. It's a death mask, right?

HARRY: Sure, death has the last word. Maybe it's all over when it's over. Maybe we all—everyone of us—have to face a hell, or the nothingness of pure emptiness; maybe we are an evolutionary mistake and death will end it all. Well, I'll tell you what you know as well as I do, religion offers hope and even the possibility of hell at least offers continued existence. Without history and religion we would have to confront our fundamental paradox because just why is there all this suffering and death? To face up to it, to this weird existence of ours, and really to try to think about it would drive anyone bonkers. No one can think it through; you've got to make some interpretation of it to adapt it to meet your own needs. Who cares if everyone interprets because whatever you can believe will do for you.

Listen, Joseph, I'll tell you something, there isn't enough rationality to solve any human problem much less the problem of existence. If no one has figured it out before us, who cares? Just get an interpretation that fits for you today. Tomorrow? Let those that come after us fix it for themselves. The fixers of today call what they do *hermeneutics,* and tomorrow they'll throw that out and use another term. So what?! If it helps us get through today. That's the real role interpretation plays, you got it?

JOSEPH: But what if there are works that don't have to be interpreted time and time again? Why not get rid of the stuff that every generation has to find new reasons for believing?

HARRY: What's so wrong with finding new reasons for keeping alive old beliefs?

JOSEPH: Are they only believed until their weaknesses become so embarrassing that they can no longer be believed? And so new ones are offered? Is it like a leaky ship that a crew has to keep repairing because no sooner do they patch up one hole than they find another leak somewhere else?

HARRY: And what doesn't need patching up?

JOSEPH: But why not just study whatever interests you without having to keep patching them up? What difference does it make if one admits that there are weaknesses in this or that system? Why expend all that effort when you know that the ship was poorly designed to begin with? Is it because it's the only ship you've heard about?

HARRY: Well, if it promises a lot, save it.

JOSEPH: But look here, suppose for a moment that these promises are the problem?

HARRY: Every system makes promises. You know that. Just mention one that doesn't need saving. Certainly, philosophy is one big saving game! All it does is find bad reasons for believing something you wish could be true. So strike up the band, play the music, march into history and fulfill your moment of destiny. Believe in God and Country, and do your duty to play out your assigned historical role as you march under this or that banner. Every institution needs saving—or interpreting if you like—because, quite frankly, there isn't enough rationality in the whole universe to insure rationality in anything that has the scope of religion, philosophy, science or the State. Maybe in heaven there is enough to go around, but not here. Man is a contradiction because Nature hasn't been able to perfect man. We are an unfinished species. So what do we do? We interpret to make the moment more palatable.

JOSEPH: Why not study without saving?

HARRY: I don't understand you. You know that? You must certainly know that philosophers spend their time interpreting! A bunch of them are trying to save your Plato, too, you know.

JOSEPH: It is not a question of saving Plato—the issue is what is involved when anyone tries to save any system. Why did it need saving? If it wasn't designed well in the first place, then why put so much belief in it? Or must you save the system by your act of believing it?

HARRY: That's a weird way of saying it. No. You are saved by believing because otherwise there wouldn't be any need to believe it. You save yourself, not the system—I mean, that's obvious.

JOSEPH: And you would go on to say that you have to believe that what's being said is true, and I imagine, that what is believed ought to be easily identified in some text? Is that right?

HARRY: You're learning. It's got to be there, simple and straightforward and literally true.

JOSEPH: Maybe, but I've found that anything that requires belief does so because it cannot be understood—so it has to be believed because what they believe they can't find in what they believe—it's not there! You know what? All the believers I've dealt with simply overlook the fact that they can't understand what they believe, but they have to believe it! And that's when the believer transforms it by interpreting it into a belief system of his own.

HARRY: You have a way of mixing up everything. But not this time. You see, new interpretations are always offered that enrich the old belief and thereby adapt it for the moment. The believer can enter into the belief because it is now joined with their own interpretations.

JOSEPH: Do you mean it can't be believed without fresh interpretations?

HARRY: You got it!

JOSEPH: Yet you also say that even these interpretations don't last, don't you? I imagine you would say that's because they are no longer believed—or understandable?

HARRY: Who cares? You've got it all wrong. Don't you understand? You don't interpret to understand, you interpret so you can believe. So what if it's not understandable? As long as you can believe it—it's believable!

JOSEPH: But if you can't understand what you believe, what makes you think you are believing it? And how do you know what you are believing? If you can't relate it to anything else you know, you can't very well make any comparisons with it, so you couldn't make analogies of it either. What would you be doing at the moment when you believe something that you can't understand the meaning of?

HARRY: You can't believe it, so you chop it.

JOSEPH: You may *believe* you *believe* that, but you don't.

HARRY: Who says so? You? That's only your view!

JOSEPH: You do believe it! You believe everything is relative so you can believe nothing is worth knowing other than your own belief.

HARRY: Listen, if you take away my belief that everything is relative, there's nothing left. Nothing at all.

JOSEPH: Then it keeps you from facing the nothingness of your position and your life.

HARRY: Who can face emptiness? You?

JOSEPH: There are other alternatives.

HARRY: No, the alternatives are only word games.

JOSEPH: Is there any interest in finding what is true?

HARRY: No, all you have are clever arguments. But the truth is that your point can be ignored, is ignored, and always will be ignored by the believer. New interpretations save the faith—that's an undeniable fact.

JOSEPH: Then aren't the newer interpretations being offered for older and weaker ones? If anything has to be interpreted, it is weak. If it is weak, why not file it away and look to something you can study directly—without the need to save it? Or if it has any merits among its weaknesses, then acknowledge that and go on. I favor studying directly and weighing carefully each idea to discover its interconnections with the other parts, to go to the basic building blocks of the system and seeing its unity. So why not set aside this saving game of interpretation, because it blocks you from learning to see what is actually there? What discipline are you mastering if every time you have a problem with the text you jump in and interpret it? What is needed is to train the mind through understanding so that it can reach for creative insights, and it is this, in turn, that matures the understanding. Of course, there is a different kind of scholarship that provides the latest fashions in interpretation that replaces previous old fashioned interpretations but–

HARRY: Joseph, you can't escape interpretation. Every historical period interpreted their history. Greeks, Romans and Koreans are each different and can't be directly compared with each other. What is good and bad in any period is relative to the time and culture. That's all there is to it. As for insights, you put too much stress on the inconsequential, that's what.

JOSEPH: Let me reflect for a moment. We still seem to be trading punches and getting nowhere. Let us consider it another way. We both agree that cultures and historical periods differ, but we differ on what to do with that difference, right? For myself, I am drawn to speculate about the differences I find among different historical periods. I wonder about what forces were at work that propelled vast development during one period and later, in a brief period of time, brought either rapid decline or produced a static and rigid society. When these differences are perceived don't they draw us to explore the reasons for such changes?

HARRY: Like what? What is it about the Greeks that makes you believe that they were better than people in other periods of history? Europe has lasted longer and done more than those little city-states of ancient Greece. But I'm not saying that Europe is better—it's just different. Because each period of history is really different than others. It's kind of simple. Each period of history is the result of tradition working itself out in the present, and that is nothing other than people in the present interpreting the past. You find yourself in a history which is nothing more than people keeping alive their interpretations of their past, and in that interpretation, you find yourself and do your understanding.

JOSEPH: Harry, isn't that view the traditional European way of looking at history?

HARRY: Sure, I suppose most Europeans would defend it. I never did get it straight, but you know what a professor of mine once said? He said that the study of political history didn't originate in Europe at all, but was an Islamic influence.

JOSEPH: Wouldn't you say this theory preserves certain European traditions?

HARRY: I would say it includes that. Maybe some of their traditions weren't historical, but— wait a minute– That doesn't make sense.

JOSEPH: Why must we study everything within a historical context? Like, what does it add?

HARRY: I'm glad you asked. Understanding takes place in history, and you can't get out of your own personal history to understand anything because you carry the interpretations of the past with you when you try to understand. You see, even if there are differences between cultures, or civilizations, none is superior to any other. Each state is within its own stage of historical development, and so the rise and fall of each state takes place within their civilization, or culture. Yet cultures have the same elements doing the same thing at different rates. That's all. Sometimes it looks like progress. Another time it's believing you are doomed. But what ties it together is nothing other than the shared beliefs of traditions, and this is what creates a common bond of feeling. You can quickly sense this when you decide who's for—or against—you.

JOSEPH: Why does that position always remind me of those other clever aphorisms? You know the ones that claim—*you can't lift yourself up by your own historical bootstraps*, or *you can't go beyond the place you were born into*, or *know your place, stay on your own side of the railroad tracks. Or take–*

HARRY: Well, it's true, isn't it? It's pretty obvious that your birth determined your historical position, and you are limited by it.

JOSEPH: Does that mean that you can't break out of those limitations by learning and experiencing other cultures? I don't suspect you mean that, or do you mean things like Christianity are dead because they came from another age and tradition? For it did emerge from a near eastern culture that was dominated by the Roman Empire.

HARRY: No, I don't mean that.

JOSEPH: Because?

HARRY: Because what started there started us, and we are still in that tradition, that's why. I know what you are going to say, but let me explain. That's why we interpret, keeping alive the old in a new form and adapting it so it doesn't die out. Systems that can't adapt die. Those that can are successful.

JOSEPH: Harry, have you ever wondered if Christianity is, in principle, weak and needs to be saved by every generation?

HARRY: Of course not. The difference adaptive systems have over others is that they have the capacity to survive. Now, that's a difference that makes a difference, right?

JOSEPH: Well, you may be right, but consider this difference and tell me what you make of it. The Greeks allegorized the mythology of Homer but neither the Australian aborigines nor the Christians could allegorize theirs.

HARRY: I don't like your comparisons, you should know that. Would you mind telling me what is so important about this idea of allegorizing?

JOSEPH: Allegories allow you to use your mind in a more profound way, that's all. When a whole culture can engage in it, then it brings about a new stage in their development. On the basis of that kind of reflection, the Greeks were able to grasp that the rational is the higher and more general expression of the mythical. They could see how the higher can be symbolized in metaphorical images, similes, and allegories, and so enjoy them both.

HARRY: So why make a big deal of that?

JOSEPH: Why? I am not quite as sure as I would like to be about this issue. But what I can say is that our religious figures and symbols have little direct relevance to my life and needs. I was a party animal long enough and began wanting to understand myself and test just how far reasoning and the use of the intellect can take me. When I made that step, I separated myself from much of my tradition. How can I put it? Because I am irresistibly drawn to the free exercise of my intelligence, and even though I know well enough that I have just begun my own seeing, I delight in the insights I have seen so far. The devotional aspects of religious life have nothing to do with my goals and are, more often than not, going along a different path than my own.

HARRY: What's happened to you? You go Plato and religion dies? Look, the Greeks had Homer, the Christians believe the Bible; to each his own. The ancient Greeks are dead; you can't resurrect them. You tell me why you would want to believe in Greek mythology? None of this makes any sense.

JOSEPH: A Hellenic, which is what the Greeks called themselves, is a state of mind not a system of beliefs. The Hellenics didn't have any split between the use of the mind and imagination. They could participate and share in the same images about the most profound aspect of life, the divine, some by using their intellect and others by using their imagination. They didn't have to sacrifice their minds or repress the imaginative side of their natures. Their epics, architecture, statuary, temples, and dramatic plays all sought to achieve an excellence that reveals in their perfection a shadow of the divine. There was never a need to either take these myths literally or historically, simply because no one would have thought they would gain salvation by believing them. Let me put it another way. No Hellenic would have said that the way to gain eternal life was to believe the Iliad.

When men use allegories, similes, and analogies to find natural parallels with their experiences, they not only become more rational but also preserve their roles in society, and they keep alive their traditions. I am most interested in exploring this issue. Doesn't this kind of inquiry interest you? I imagine it would, since you hold that understanding takes place in history.

HARRY: I'm not sure about all this, it seems to have gotten all messed up. But for me, they're just different! I'll never figure out why anyone would waste their time trying to classify Greek mythology as a religion. As far as I can see, it is not even a– a genuine religious expression—much less a religion.

ELEA: They're not just different to me, Harry. I'd like to see what's behind that point Joseph made about allegorizing. Are you saying that the cultures that could allegorize their mythologies have a significantly different development than those that couldn't?

JOSEPH: Yes. The Jews didn't have to model their thought and actions on a jealous, angry, and tribal deity after Philo showed them how the old testament could be allegorized. Philo did for the Bible what the ancient Greeks did to Homer. But Christians resist allegorizing their myth and so they can't break out of static forms, so there is little chance for them to develop an appreciative understanding of systems or theories of reality beyond forms.

ELEA: And how do you see allegorizing does that?

JOSEPH: Since allegorizing, in its perfect form, is the art that tells a story in one set of terms but its meaning must be discovered in another parallel set of terms, it allows the perception of a higher more rational form behind a more primitive expression.

ELEA: What do you call a perfect allegory? I mean what would be an example of a perfect allegory?

JOSEPH: One of the greatest allegories is Plato's allegory of the cave and the upper world, found in the seventh book of the Republic. The meaning of each term and its relationship to all the others in that allegory can be found within the Republic itself. Thus, it provides an easy way to test your understanding of the work as a whole.

ELEA: That's interesting, but what does it do? I mean, if you ignore it, as I did when I read it, what have you really lost?

JOSEPH: Lost? With it you have to consciously search out all the parallel terms and then you can systematically reconcile all the parts into a splendid unity. If you do it, you will learn what understanding a dialogue is all about. More than this, it will also bring you to the curious task of working out the relationships between the Good and the Idea of the Good, and that is something that I have found to be very challenging.

ELEA: This may be a dumb question, but how does that relate to philosophy?

JOSEPH: The journey to the Idea of the Good—which, by the way, is described as the most brilliant light of Being—is the royal road that the philosopher travels, and gaining that vision is the practice of philosophy. But there is still more. You see, once that has been seen, one knows it as ultimate reality, and from that lofty vision one is said to be able to go on to grasp the nature of the Good itself through the mastery of the dialectic.

ELEA: I haven't the faintest idea of what you are talking about, but it sounds wonderful. But that brings me to ask why you used Plato's allegory instead of selecting one from Philo? Is one better than the other?

JOSEPH: Yes. There is a fundamental difference between the way Philo and Plato use allegory. For the structure of Plato's Republic was designed to be expressed through allegory, analogies and similes, but Philo inherited a work that had no such design. He tried to allegorize it in every way; however, it had an intrinsic weakness. Clearly, there is much in the Garden of Eden myth that can be allegorized, and Philo, indeed, does it, but the key relationship between God and man, the creator and the created, has inherent difficulties when it is allegorized.

ELEA: But I thought you said all myths can be allegorized.

JOSEPH: They might be, but when some myths are allegorized they can't be believed! To save them for belief, parts of a myth may be rejected or transformed by arbitrary interpretations. In a similar way, when actual events can't be reconciled with one's expectations then another myth may be created to save the belief. Now, I know that sounds curious but it is true. I learned to work on several myths, allegories, satires, and analogies—and it was as much fun as it was revealing.

ELEA: And are you saying that when some myths are allegorized they can't be believed? Give me one that couldn't be believed! I'd like to see one.

JOSEPH: Will you accept the biblical story of the Garden of Eden as a myth? That's one that Philo explores.

ELEA: Sure.

JOSEPH: First, though, it would be helpful if we could add another dimension to this inquiry because I just saw how it can fit into what we have been discussing. So try this question. Were you taught that God banished both Adam and Eve from the Garden of Eden?

ELEA: Yes, as I recall they were thrown out and forced to work by the sweat of their brow from that day on for disobeying God's command not to eat the fruit of the Tree of Good and Evil.

JOSEPH: Actually, you are not reporting the myth but an interpretation of it. According to the myth, while both Adam and Eve had eaten from the Tree of the Knowledge of Good and Evil, God only exiled Adam—not Eve—and only from the garden—but not from Eden. The reason God gives for the exile is not because Adam ate from the Tree of the Knowledge of Good and Evil, but to keep him from eating the fruit of the Tree of Life; for if Adam had, that would mean that he would become like a god with eternal life. Thus, the central theme or lesson of the myth is that God banishes those who might become like him, either in the knowledge of good and evil or eternal life.

ELEA: That is very interesting—very. God made us in his image and likeness and punishes us for realizing it? Now that is immensely strange.

JOSEPH: Yes, Philo's allegory ignored this theme. He skipped over it because he couldn't find a parallel for that capricious act in any rational structure. The myth reports a jealous and unjust God using punishment arbitrarily. It is strange because he prohibits what he has created in his own "image and likeness" from becoming like himself in the most significant way. Faced with this difficulty, most authorities prefer to either ignore the end of the story and interpret the objectionable parts of the myth rather than face this issue by systematically allegorizing its message.

ELEA: That's a very strict way of understanding and it's kind of sad to see it that way because it means that if God is as you just described him, then man is doomed because he is flawed in the most fundamental way, doesn't it? Since he was created in the image and likeness of an irrational God, then both the creator and the created are flawed! Maybe we shouldn't take it so literally, so strictly.

JOSEPH: If not this way, then what way? If it's there, then read it the way it is written.

ELEA: Well, anyway, let me thank you for your account. But I'll tell you that's not the way I recall the Garden of Eden story. What if I go back and look it up and prove you wrong? Then, what will you say?

JOSEPH: That would be fine, but the book is not going to change, Elea. It will say what it says for you, me, anyone else who cares to look it up.

ELEA: Goodness, you're pretty dogmatic, aren't you?

JOSEPH: No, but I can understand how it seems that way to you because interpretation blocks understanding. It is not easy to read something that has been distorted by years of interpretation. After that you'll read into it what you expect to be there. I had to go through what you are now facing, but go ahead because it's worth going through. The real question is what will you do if the way I just reported it is there, you know, literally there?

ELEA: I really don't know.

JOSEPH: Then, I can expect you will want to verify it for yourself, won't you? You'll get the book, open it up, look it up, and conclude, right?

ELEA: Yes, I guess I'll have to, now. But wait a minute, didn't you mention another case where a myth is invented but taken literally? What's that one? Or shouldn't I ask?

JOSEPH: I think you will agree that when you read the Gospel accounts of the resurrection, those that say that Jesus physically died and returned were those that were written from ten to thirty years after the fall of Jerusalem and the destruction of the temple.
     First, would you agree that biblical prophets and the early Christians believed that the end of everything and the beginning of heavenly rule was supposed to coincide with the fall of Jerusalem and the destruction of the temple?

ELEA: Yes, I think Paul believed he would witness that in his own lifetime.

JOSEPH: And were you also taught that Mark, the earliest gospel, was written at the time of the fall and reports that since the end was imminent believers were urged to prepare for it?

ELEA: I'm not sure if I was taught that, but I was taught that Jesus died, was resurrected, and will return to judge sinners. But

Christians are still waiting for that to happen, so the end wasn't as imminent as Mark thought.

JOSEPH: Well, that prediction did fail, but the important thing is that Mark didn't say anything about a physical resurrection of Jesus because he believed the end was just around the corner.

ELEA: Sure he did—didn't he?

JOSEPH: If you look at the conclusion of Mark's gospel you will see it ends at Chapter 16, Verse 8, and all the rest—some twelve verses—were added many years later. That meant that Bibles dated in the early third century don't have any reference to a resurrection in the gospel of Mark, and they all end at 16:8; and the gospels that do include it were written much later.

ELEA: Oh! I see what you're saying. If the end of the world was happening today or tomorrow there would be no need for a physical resurrection.

HARRY: Oh! You see what's going on—how nice! Would you mind sharing that with me?!

ELEA: It's really kind of obvious, Harry. The early Christians believed that the world would come to an end after the fall of Jerusalem, but it didn't come off.

HARRY: So what?!

ELEA: The resurrection account was only added to the gospels after it was clear to everyone that the prophecy failed.

HARRY: So what? It failed—so what?

ELEA: Then what kept alive the belief?

HARRY: What did, Miss Elea?!

ELEA: Only a divine being could be resurrected from the dead and if he promised he would return at the end of the world, then you had better believe it! So they added a greater belief to save the lesser, isn't that it, Joseph?

JOSEPH: Say, that is a good way to express it, Elea. Maybe that's why the gospels after Mark had to build the theme that Jesus was the Son of God.

ELEA: You know, this is kind of exciting and scary. There is something strange about someone being resurrected after being dead for three days.

JOSEPH: But the resurrection appearances weren't physical. The authors of the later gospels wrote their accounts in such a way that they can be read as a nonphysical event. Now, I know a lot of people interpret it to mean a physical resurrection, but there is no need to do that. If you just read it you can see what's going on there.

HARRY: Wait just a minute. I'm not sure where this is going. I thought you were going to give the argument that one of my profs often used. You know that the resurrection theme created the need for the church and that those who were granted an appearance of Jesus, the risen Christ, were naturally chosen to be the leaders of the church. But you are saying something else, aren't you?

ELEA: Yes, I was—and he may be right, but I wasn't thinking about that. Joseph, were you saying that the other gospels were written later than Mark?

JOSEPH: True enough. The gospels that are assumed to mention a physical resurrection were written about ten to twenty years after the fall of Jerusalem, or 70 A.D., which was 50 to 70 years after the death of Jesus.

ELEA: And during those years after the fall of Jerusalem and the destruction of the temple, it must have become painfully obvious that the prophecy failed since there was no end—it wasn't happening and wasn't going to happen.

JOSEPH: Well, since it didn't happen they had to accept that they were wrong. Their sense of superiority and certainty were shaken. They didn't have anything to believe.

ELEA: Well, you couldn't believe something was going to happen that *didn't* happen, but you might believe it *may* happen if you've got something that dwarfs that belief and follows from it. That's for sure.

JOSEPH: And along comes the gospels of Matthew, Luke, and John—and then there really was something momentous to believe in—the resurrection of Jesus—and with it, the announcement that the second coming will occur sometime in the immediate future.

ELEA: And then there was something to believe and they had their myth. No, actually it's an interlocking belief, isn't it? Since one reinforces the other. I never thought of the resurrection like this before.

JOSEPH: Okay, then let me add something else. There were some who claimed that the resurrection was not a literal happening but something to be understood, analogically, as symbolic. As I recall, it has been said that resurrection—is to the life that has died—as spiritual resurrection—is to the life that knows the divine light. This kind of knowing, of course, is also called enlightenment. It has also been said that those that can accept that the divine was and is the divine light know the personification of that light is Jesus—which is what he said he was.

ELEA: I don't know. This is getting clear and confusing at the same time. But if it can be understood in that way, just where is the need for belief? However, Joseph, I am not sure how all this fits together. I guess I will have to nail it down for myself. I think it might be good to see it clearly, but I'm not sure I want to. I mean— I want to, but I'm not sure where it's going.

JOSEPH: Elea, you have a good mind for this kind of reflection. So you have to put up with uncertainty, so what? You have shown you enjoy doing it. Where is the problem?

ELEA: I guess it is kind of strange. I am attracted to it because it's part me and my past, but I don't want to fall for any easy trip again. Don't say it. I know I'm not as clear as I'd like to be, but, Joseph, what do you do with this kind of understanding? Like— where does it go? And where do you take it?

JOSEPH: Elea, when you read other religions it's a lot easier to understand one of them. You can see how to understand them symbolically.

HARRY: Symbolically! That's a good one. Everybody can play symbolic games and you got nothing. The resurrection was physical! There is nothing you can say that can convince me that that fact wasn't established by multiple witnesses. You know it. I know it. Do you want to become like those nuts who take everything symbolically? Where everybody plays by their own rules? Everyone ends up with nothing they can believe. But if you can't make it into something you have to believe, you ain't got nothing. Sure enough, it's that simple. Believe it and you're saved. If you can't, that leaves you out! Philosophy, reason, meditation and all the other stuff won't help you. You can't prepare for it, can't get ready for it, can't wait until you're good enough, prayed enough—nope! There is only one thing and that is to jump in! You got to take the plunge right now. Enlightenment won't help you. Nothing will. That's all there is to it.

JOSEPH: When I was in class we explored that issue and compared every reference. You really might enjoy doing it.

HARRY: So when you put it together what did it look like?

JOSEPH: You can put it many ways, I guess, but it's clear that his appearance after the resurrection was not physical because he wasn't visible to everyone. If anything is physical then everyone can see it. Whoever can see sees what's visible—if they aren't blind they can see it. But the appearances of Jesus aren't like that; if he wanted you to see him, you did—otherwise you did not. Each of the gospel writers except Mark carries this theme.

ELEA: I think I see what you're doing, Joseph. You're gathering together each of those sections in the text and making up a theory that can include them all.

JOSEPH: That's right. A theory stands until someone can take those same parts and weave them into something else that fits the parts better. And that, Harry, leads to the conclusion that the resurrection was not physical.

HARRY: I don't believe it! It's like you're saying—no, that is what
            you're saying—that they made up a punishing belief! That's like
            what my Dad would say to end our crying, "If you don't stop cry-
            ing I'll really give you something to cry about!" You're unbeliev-
            able!

JOSEPH: Well, that shows you can't believe everything.

HARRY: I can believe anything I want to believe!

JOSEPH: Didn't you just say something was unbelievable? Aren't
            you saying that there is something unbelievable?

HARRY: Okay, I'll play it your way. You did say, didn't you, that
            the parts have to fit together? Didn't you? It's not that you're wrong.
            That's not what this is all about. It's that you are blind to what's out
            there in the real world. You're kind of stupid. Now, don't get all
            steamed up. You got a stupid theory, and the only damn way you
            could put it together is to ignore what every kid in Sunday school
            knows. Everyone knows the way Jesus dealt with skepticism and
            doubt but you. Haven't you heard of Doubting Thomas? Sure, he
            doubted and Jesus made him stick his fingers into his open wounds
            to prove he had been resurrected, and that means physically, and
            that means having a body. Now deal with that fact, or are you
            going to be clever and deny the historicity of the story and argue it
            never took place because you can't deal with it? Now, dear old
            buddy, it's there—deal with it. Don't interpret it away; as you would
            say, just read it. That's all that I have to say.

JOSEPH: Well, I know what you are going through, at least some-
            what, because I went through it, too. Maybe we start off differ-
            ently because I read to discover what's there not to confirm what I
            already believe. I've sweated over Doubting Thomas many a time.
            You'll have to figure it out and puzzle through it yourself.

HARRY: Puzzle over it? There's nothing to puzzle over! It is right
            there to be believed. I know you. You just puzzle over this stuff to
            keep from believing. That's all there is to it. Just answer me one
            thing. How comes it that you ignored the one fact that can throw
            out your lousy theory? Go ahead, Joseph, I'm waiting. Or am I
            supposed to wonder about what's obvious?

JOSEPH: I'll tell you why I think the story is still open to understanding Jesus' appearance as spiritual and not physical.

HARRY: I'll bet you, *you* can't make it come off.

JOSEPH: Would you say physical objects can't go through doors?
If doors are said to be shut and yet if someone appears in front of
you, then apart from some trick, that appearance couldn't be physical, could it?

HARRY: What makes you think that's what happened? That's not
in the story and you know damn well it's not! It's not as I recall it!

JOSEPH: You better reread it then, Harry, because it is there. And,
by the way, Thomas didn't put his fingers into the wound either.

HARRY: I don't have to reread a damn thing. I know what I believe. You start with doubt and look for every loophole in the story
to read into it your own lousy theory.

JOSEPH: It is not a loophole.

HARRY: You mean that Jesus just appeared in front of the them?
Jesus didn't, wouldn't have, and couldn't have done that kind of
thing. You're lost.

JOSEPH: He sure did. In Luke's account of his appearance before
his disciples they were so frightened when he stood among them
that they thought he was a spirit and–

HARRY: You know what? You know too much! There's a story
about people like you who quote scripture, you know?

JOSEPH: You know where you can go, don't you?

ELEA: If I'm not interrupting something, I would like to get
back to what you said, Joseph. Maybe you're right about all of this
but I'm not sure you answered my question. I'll tell you what,
before I can go any further, I'll have to do my homework on this.
But, thanks. I thought I had a question, but I guess I don't.

JOSEPH: Okay, and when you do, be sure to include Bultmann's works on demythologizing Christianity and Maccoby's book, *The Mythmaker*.

HARRY: Bultmann! Elea, do you know what this guy is suggesting? I'll tell you what's behind his simple reading assignment, but maybe you just don't care. I can't figure you out anymore either—I guess everything changes, even you! Anyway, Bultmann's so-called demythologizing is nothing short of eliminating everything that doesn't pass as a respectable fact in a high school science test.

ELEA: Like what?

HARRY: I heard of Bultmann at UCSB. I can't recall all of it, but he showed what most of us call the Christian doctrine was mythological because it was unscientific. You know it. It goes something like, Jesus-is-the-only-begotten-Son-of-God, the atonement for man's sins, who will return on the clouds of heaven to redeem his believers, and deprive the demonic forces of their power, etcetera, etcetera. These, of course, are very unscientific beliefs. I never asked you, Elea, but what do you make of it? Where do you stand?

ELEA: So, Joseph, that's what Bultmann calls a myth! For me, Harry, Christianity has always been something I've heard around the house and maybe believed, but now the very notion of it turns me off. I'll tell you why. The whole picture of a God destroying everything so he can give eternal life to those who believe he is God and sending those who don't believe it to an eternal Hell is not my idea of an adequate reason to destroy the entire cosmos, and that goes double when you figure out the reason he rewards some and punishes others. Like, why would a God who rules over an entire universe with countless galaxies—each of which has countless suns which, in turn, have their own planets rotating around them—be so upset over whether or not his son is believed by some creatures to be a God? Like, would a creator God ignore the good and evil his creatures do and judge their worth solely in terms of whether or not they believe something about his son? No, I don't have it yet. I'd like to express it better, but I don't have it in the words I'd like to—yet.

JOSEPH: Perhaps, but you do have a keen appreciation for justice, Elea. I like seeing that. Ever get into the idea of Justice in Plato's *Republic*?

ELEA: I've heard it's more than each doing their own thing. But, as for Bultmann, if that is what he calls mythology, then what's the issue?

JOSEPH: The issue is whether or not those very beliefs can be found in the gospels. Now, if they're not there, what difference does it make? Well, for one thing they are only in Paul's writings. Paul's writings had been around for years before the gospels were written. Did those later writers knowingly ignore Paul's gospel and stress something entirely different? One way or the other, there is a problem, isn't there? Paul didn't include any of the teachings of Jesus in his gospel, and the gospel writers ignore, at least for the most part, the message of Paul.

ELEA: So now I know a bit of Bultmann, but what about Maccoby? Come on, Joseph, how do they relate?

JOSEPH: If you want it in a nutshell, Maccoby shows that since you can't find Paul's message in the other gospels and they came later, it is important to discover where his message came from. You can say Maccoby demythologizes—not Christianity—but Paul, hence the title: *The Mythmaker*.

ELEA: Whoa! That is heavy! Then Paul made up the myth others call Christianity. That's interesting. I've never thought of studying Christianity the way you have. You are suggesting, aren't you, that we look at it just as it is in itself, and make contrasts back and forth as if each of these New Testament writers were arguing for their own positions? I have to admit that sounds like an exciting way to study. And, at the same time, you puzzle through analogies, allegories, parables, and whatnot. At this point, I don't know whether it should be believed as a myth, or *de*-mythed, understood or believed or–

HARRY: Christian belief is not a myth. Did you hear me?

JOSEPH: If it is a myth, call it a myth. A myth has three elements, first, there must be players—and at least one must be of divine origin; second, there must be a drama; and finally there must be a setting or place where the action takes place. If these elements are present then it is fair to call it a myth.

HARRY: But it is not mythical! I'll tell you something else, it is easy to criticize—anybody can do it. But there are people who resent people like you who chop their religion. Another thing, there are a lot of people whose lives would be worthless without their belief. That's right! If they couldn't cling to their belief they would have nothing. Sure, you can call it a myth, but it's not a myth to a believer. So what do you gain by all this?

          Your clever way of understanding leaves nothing for belief. It's you that doesn't understand. You haven't understood that what is needed is not an understandable belief but a belief you don't need to understand, only believe. It's belief that saves—not understanding.

JOSEPH: Harry, when you are interested in exploring ideas do you first separate out those you want to protect?

HARRY: Now, look Joseph, Elea over there may not know what you're driving at, but I do. Take the myth out of Christianity and you got nothing. That's the scholars' way of attacking Paul's position. You guys all want to take Paul out of the Bible. I've heard it discussed before at SB. Why can't you just leave well enough alone?

JOSEPH: Is the question too difficult to deal with? Consider it this way, if Paul has a teaching that is not found in the other gospels, and he does call his teachings his gospel, so—why believe Paul rather than Jesus?

          You see, Harry, the question is not trivial. It asks if Jesus clearly and unambiguously gave the requirements to become one of his followers and for gaining eternal life, and if Paul gives another set of requirements that are altogether different, then why would anyone who claims to follow Jesus, follow Paul?

HARRY: Baloney, Joseph, nothing but baloney! You know damn well what all this means. You do know, don't you, that Paul got his teaching from Jesus, "not from any man," as he says—so what you're saying is nonsense. On the road to Damascus he had one hell of a conversion experience. That's what started him off. He had a real Christian light experience and all the rest is pagan, oriental mishmash—New Age bunco.

JOSEPH: You are trying to mix oil and wine, Harry. Paul never claimed to have had a major conversion experience; it was Luke who claimed that Paul had a conversion experience. Compare each point that Paul makes in Galatians about his experience and his teachings and examine what Luke says in Acts about that conversion experience. There are three references in Luke; check and compare them and you'll find they can't be reconciled. Indeed, Luke wrote around 85 A.D. and interpreted what he believed must have been Paul's experience. However, it must have occurred some fifty years earlier. But Paul never claimed that he had the experience that Luke describes. Why does Luke say that Paul had an experience that Paul himself never said he had? Surely, the most compelling argument against Luke's version is merely to reflect on the significance it would have had for Paul, if he had mentioned it. When you consider the significance of those experiences it is altogether impossible to understand—if Paul had such experiences—why he never mentioned them in his letters or preaching; for Paul was always intent on establishing his authority with others.

HARRY: What makes you think it could never have happened? How can you sit there and say what you do? You weren't there—Luke was.

JOSEPH: No, he wasn't. He says he compiled his account from studying other sources, but he wasn't an eye witness. Why would an eye witness copy 60% of Mark's gospel? Assume Paul had the experience that Luke describes and ask yourself: Why would that event have been ignored by Paul? What reason would he have, or anyone else for that matter, for not mentioning it in his talks, especially those he had with the apostles of Jesus? If he told them, don't you think it would have been included in the epistles by at least one of the Apostles before Luke mentions it? Paul said he didn't receive his direction or gospel from any man, yet Luke said that after Paul's light experience he was given his mission by Ananias. Further, did–

HARRY: Wait a minute! You've got it all backward; it wasn't the light that made that experience great. That's not the point; it was the message of Jesus that transformed him. The religious life for Christians starts and ends with the cross—not Edison. The fact is, as I heard at SB, experiencing light experiences without Jesus starts a fire that pagans burning in hell will see.

JOSEPH: That doesn't sound like something you learned at UCSB.

HARRY: So what?!

ELEA: Joseph, would you mind filling me in on the issue here? You two are just winding each other up.

JOSEPH: Behind our talk is an issue, all right. Mircea Eliade reports that some meditating monks on Mount Anthos were so spiritually advanced into the divine luminosity that at night their caves shone with such intensity that they were visible from a considerable distance. In our own time, one night a few years ago, Sai Baba went through a similar experience on a mountain top where his followers witnessed his radiance which was also said to have been visible from quite a distance. Elea, consider what you would say if you were to see someone transformed by divine light so much so that their face shone like the sun, that their very garments were so penetrated by that light that they were as white as light itself?

ELEA: Do I get you right? Are you saying that there is some evidence out there that claims some religious experiences are so intense that they produce that? I guess that's what you're saying all right. I'll tell you that *that* is something I am even having difficulty imagining, *but* if I knew it did occur, I wouldn't be the same person I am now—that's for sure.

JOSEPH: What if you were among those who were led up the mountain that night to witness Jesus, Moses, and Elijah bathed in that light? Would you regard that as a worthy object of speculation? Recall that Moses led his people out of their captivity and gave them the commandments while Elijah was said to be able to restore all things. Now, if this took place, is it not likely that you might wonder about the meaning of this transformation experience and why Moses and Elijah were included in it? For an everyday existence was transcended in a radiant transformation into the divine. Consider, is this not rising from a life which, by contrast, is dead? Because participating in this way into the divine deserves the name Son of Man. You can say that's what it means.

ELEA: Well, for one thing, I would say that that happening would be worth a thousand miracles. I guess it is one of the stories about Jesus, but I never heard of it. What do you *do* with it? I mean, how can you study that kind of thing?

JOSEPH: How? Compare and contrast, that's how.

ELEA: Is that how you studied Christianity? Comparatively?

JOSEPH: Yes. I had a class at GWC and we used Aland's *Synopsis of the Four Gospels*, Kee's study of the gospels, and Perrin's *Intro*.... They were real good works. And we used a work book the instructor put together.

ELEA: I would like to get into something like that. Another thing, are there records of people having that kind of experience from different traditions?

JOSEPH: Reports of these experiences occur from Plato to Tibetan Philosophy, from Korean Buddhism to Hinduism, from Chinese philosophy to Shamanism, to mention only some traditions. For myself, I find that by studying and reflecting on similar stories you gain an appreciation of the greatness of the figures who experienced them, an insight into the nature of reality, and the need to fashion your own philosophy so that it will be broad enough to contain room for everything that's meaningful.

ELEA: But what does it mean to Christianity?

JOSEPH: Biblical authorities call that event the parousia (παρουσία).

ELEA: I'm not sure what to say.

HARRY: You may not be sure, but I am. It's just what I thought. You start out by getting people to study comparative religions, and then you steer them into philosophy to make everything seem right, don't you?

JOSEPH: I am having enough trouble steering myself through this philosophical journey, and you believe I'm leading others? If others want to go along for the ride, that's fine, but I'm not proselytizing. It may seem different to you but that's the way it is. I'm still new at this game and haven't done all my homework on all those religions and philosophies, but I do intend to explore them more fully sometime. There are people around here, and you know some of them, who enjoy exploring these ideas—so you could fit right in.

HARRY: You know what? You've got to be kidding. I don't believe you. You confuse the everyday person and attract the bright ones into your philosophy, don't you? I'm not sure I can say what you get out of it but I know what effect it has.

    All you're trying to do is to wreck the lives of believers. You don't really care one way or the other. You take the best and show it's not unique. You even make believe there are modern Jesus types, don't you? You know what else you do? You look for contradictions in order to get others to deny their faith. You sound like someone interested in saving the true faith, but that's crap. I've heard it all before. What you really do is rub those contradictions into the nose of believers, like people disciplining their dogs, they rub their noses in it. But what they're really doing is having sadistic fun and feeling smug and superior.

    The truth is that believers have something that you nonbelievers envy. You can't force it; it has to move you, and when it does you can get good feelings out of it and group acceptance too.

JOSEPH: Perhaps, but I don't think so. Which of these teachings attracts and magnifies neurotic tendencies that undermine the use of the mind, and which allows for personal growth as it enhances the use of understanding? You will agree, one creates divisions and dissensions while the other assists in unifying mankind, won't you?

HARRY: How noble you make it sound with your two possibilities. The point is that there is plenty of stuff around to criticize— why direct it at something that serves a deep emotional need? If you can't join it, why chop it? I don't believe in Santa Claus, but I don't go around undermining believers of it.

JOSEPH: Do you also give the same advice when they in turn become political and insist that their values become the law of the land? Do you also caution them when they become hostile to other forms of religious expression?

HARRY: You hide behind questions like a kid behind his mother's skirt. Why don't you just say what you think? Afraid? Aren't you and those like you really afraid of being labeled the Anti-Christ?

JOSEPH: Is that all it takes? Merely by differing from an interpretation accepted by the many you become the Anti-Christ? But I will answer you, Harry, when you figure out what Christ means, then I'll bet you'll see something worth seeing.

HARRY: What?

JOSEPH: Then you will be surprised who really are the Anti-Christs.

HARRY: That, Oh-Make-Believe-Professor, is nothing other than bull. And it is an insult! All you do is pile it on higher and deeper.

JOSEPH: If you want to understand, you have to see for yourself.

HARRY: It just dawned on me what's wrong. When you study the Bible in college you lose your faith because you guys learn from rationalists, not Christians.

JOSEPH: Learning is what you get after the critical thinking is over.

HARRY: Oh, God, another critical thinking course!

JOSEPH: Well, if you want to learn, you first have to see the issue and then squeeze the answers out of the text. But it is not easy because you have to pass through perplexity and doubt. That's inevitable if understanding is to be reached.

HARRY: You know why I won't go through the effort? I won't because there is no need to! I already have an interpretation. So it's not going to prove anything. Your conclusions wouldn't be the only ones to draw anyway. So why don't we just skip this topic? It's only your interpretation anyway.
    Say, waiter, I do believe I need another cup of coffee. Thanks.

EURIPIDES: Anyone else care for another cup? Or anything else?

HARRY: No, we only need coffee. Elea, what are you really getting out of all this?

ELEA: For me, it's getting simpler. I'm trying to sort out a lot of things and get clear about all this. You see, I've thought I've known things when I didn't and believed I understood something I was reading when I was actually interpreting something into it that wasn't there. I thought something was there that wasn't, and now I'm finally beginning to enjoy something I believed I had rejected. Now I'll tell you something, Harry, if this is critical thinking, I'm for learning more of it.

HARRY: But why are you getting into it? You don't really care about being a Christian, do you?

ELEA: When I rejected it I didn't have good reasons so I just ignored it. Now, I can understand it in a new way without rejecting it!

HARRY: That's crazy! You mean you want to interpret it so you don't have to believe it?

JOSEPH: Or maybe she can read it to get out of interpreting it. And, isn't this whole business of interpreting just another way of saying everything is relative to the interpreter?

HARRY: What's that?

JOSEPH: Doesn't it look like you either have to *believe* an interpretation or *understand* what you read?

HARRY: All you need is belief. If you believe what Christians believe is in the book, then you're a Christian, and that's whether or not you think it's there.

JOSEPH: Then are you a Christian if you believe something that's not even said in the gospels? What does it mean if you believe what isn't there? Can't you be a Christian and also be a good reader and understand what you are reading?

HARRY: I imagine you can read anything you want into it or out of it—if you want.

Say, Waiter, are you used to this kind of talking going on around here?

EURIPIDES: When his crowd comes in here, they do plenty of talking. They even talk through their banquets. They talk, talk, talk.

[INTERLUDE]

PART THREE

HARRY: Well, Joseph, it seems to me that you've learned to argue well, but I'll still tell you something. Who cares if you believe my theory is inadequate or not? It's still what I feel is true, and no one will ever be able to show me, at least to my satisfaction, that my experience is not real for me. You believe you caught my system in a contradiction, but it's easy to get rid of your objection. I won't call it a theory, so it's not a philosophy. It's just what it is, and that ought to be enough for anyone, even for you.

JOSEPH: It's not what I think that determines all this. If anyone claims that their experience is real and their statements about their experience are infallible, then they are making a claim of knowledge. If it is found to be inadequate, like yours, then they may have a point of view, but that's not a philosophy.

ELEA: So what if it's not a philosophy—why are you dwelling on that?

JOSEPH: That's a good question. Harry, don't look for a con, it's not a con. This kind of philosophy challenges us to play on a higher level of thought than we have in the past. I'll tell you what it is— it's an invitation, not merely to explore higher questions and specu- late on this or that but to investigate the possibility that you may be able to reach more profound levels of existence. What do you think—not believe? Do you want to play a new game? There is a new game in town.

HARRY: Has anyone ever told you that many people don't deny that you guys may experience these profound levels of existence, but the suspicion is that it's likely the result of some drug trip or some subjective neurotic trip. I'm not saying some of you guys may not experience what you call profound levels of existence, but what I will tell you is that it doesn't amount to much. You can't point to one dope head whose life is better because he tripped out, and that goes double for those of you who have overactive imaginations. You know why? It's because the action is here not in some lofty airy realm.

JOSEPH: You can judge experience independent of how you got there. You can get there by car, walking, prayer, meditation, and drugs. What is important is what you learn from what you do—whatever you do.

ELEA: Whatever you do? Well, some people get off doing one thing and some another. You go for knowledge so you're drawn to these issues, but for me, I believe we've gone too far with knowledge. For me I feel we should use our minds and spend our energy on saving our planet, protecting the environment. You know, if we achieve peace that will end the arms race, and if we end the arms race that will put an end to most scientific projects. Scientific knowledge, weapons for war, and the destruction of the environment all go together. Personally, I find knowledge boring. I took the math and science classes and got good grades, but when I look back on it, all I can say is that science discovers some interesting patterns, but all it really does is find the nuts and bolts that tie stuff together. So what? You know what I mean? There's not enough in it for me. Now, if you think I'm off base tell me how.

JOSEPH: Those aren't the issues I deal with. I am very puzzled about many issues concerning the origin of belief.

ELEA: Like what?

JOSEPH: While I like your questions I am more concerned with–Why do we get locked up into beliefs if wisdom is so great? Why is it that we can have beliefs that are so powerful they block our development, and yet we don't even know we have them? Where does it get that kind of power? If we could answer these questions could our schools help expose these beliefs and eliminate their effect?

ELEA: So these are the questions you guys explore together?

JOSEPH: No, there are other questions more complex or interesting than these.

ELEA: Like?

JOSEPH: Whether or not knowledge is one or many, and, if many, does it admit of various kinds of knowledge.

ELEA: I can't even imagine going around with a question like that on my mind. So that's what you call being philosophical!

JOSEPH: Not quite. That's being philosophically pregnant, and when it reaches a maturity it might require a philosophical midwife.

ELEA: Shall I presume, Dr. Livingston, that you will lead us to the discovery of what philosophical midwifery is and give us the signs of being philosophically pregnant?

JOSEPH: With that question I'll introduce you to Platonic thought. When Socrates asked a bright young man, named Theaetetus, to find a single formula that grasps the many kinds of knowledge into one, Theaetetus described the state of mind that question put him in. He said:
"But I assure you Socrates, I have often set myself to study that problem, when I heard reports of the questions you ask. But I cannot persuade myself that I can give any satisfactory solution or that anyone has ever stated in my hearing the sort of answer you require. And yet I cannot get the question out of my mind."(Cornford, 24)
Socrates calls that state of mind being philosophically pregnant.

ELEA: Thanks. That's some state! I will have fun figuring out exactly how many points are in that quote, but one thing is clear enough: Theaetetus doesn't have the question—the question has him! Neither Harry nor I have been pregnant like that! As a matter of fact, I doubt that I've ever met anyone pregnant in that sense of the word. How do you figure that? Somehow, we've lost something, haven't we?

JOSEPH: Well, Elea, that is not easy to answer. I think we have
been convinced that there are narrow limits to what we can know;
any attempt to go beyond the common sense view is scorned so
that the study of metaphysics is dismissed as irrelevant. Plenty of
teachers have tried to persuade us to become junior scientists, but
how many encouraged us to learn philosophy? What's worse is
that nearly everyone I knew linked Catholic thought with metaphysics and the Dark ages; so up springs images in their minds of
religious bigotry and intolerance——with its religious wars, inqui-
sitions, and the total suppression of non-Christian cultures. So
metaphysics was seen, or is still seen, as justifying and supporting
that blood bath. Among the people I know, most prefer to keep the
lid on the box; better to ignore all that and hope history won't
repeat itself in your life time.

HARRY: Sure, we have achieved a lot without metaphysics, so we
don't need it.

JOSEPH: That does express it, Harry. It's difficult to show metaphysics is relevant for today, especially when it is not introduced
in the schools. The vacuum this creates allows an easy victory for
pragmatism and skepticism.

HARRY: So what? So what if these are ideas that apply to everything? All I get is a lecture on history. Okay, I'll be its defender.
Christianity was merely a reflection of the corrupt historical period of which it was a part. You are too quick to blame it, I'd say.
Or are you like Gibbon's *Rise and Fall* and blame Christianity for
the fall of the Roman Empire? And what's so damn special about
saving Platonism? And another thing, are you going to defend
drugs, too? Learn from everything, *even drugs?* Bravery from a
bottle, wisdom from grass? Anyway, maybe Christianity brought
about the fall of Rome. For all I know, maybe it did, but I bet if we
fall it'll be because people are hooked on dope. We both know
guys who went searching for the experiences, and look at them;
they are just shells of their old self. Sad and depressing to see
them again. So you know what? Go ahead and tell me– What's so
special about saving Platonism?

JOSEPH: You have made a lot of points, and you have some good questions, Harry. Let me first say something about Platonism—at least as I know it. Wisdom traditions function in a very special way. They furnish us with maps for reaching and integrating the most profound levels of experience. Buddhism, Hinduism, and other traditions served that purpose in the East, while Platonic tradition served that purpose in the West. If you ever decide to do it—and by that I mean practice Platonic philosophy—you will soon discover the need for something like a map to chart your direction and progress. And the contemplative path of the Platonic tradition expresses itself through metaphysics, so that too has to be mastered. The real challenge is to master it, teach it, and add to it.

HARRY: You mean to tell me that some people are still doing that?

JOSEPH: Yes, some people still use it that way, but it's not taught or practiced as a contemplative path in academia. Common sense pragmatism and Christianity was, and still is, hostile to the wisdom traditions and–

HARRY: There you go again, knocking Christianity. I knew you had fooled around with Buddhism—wait a minute! You know what you are?! You're a relic from the past, that's what! You're a pagan philosopher!

JOSEPH: You got it, Harry. To do philosophy is to be Hellenic. And as they say, the highest flower of Hellenic thought is Platonic philosophy.

ELEA: Wait a minute, Harry, remember, you turned the discussion over to me.

HARRY: And I couldn't be more pleased to turn it over to you. I didn't get one lecture from Joseph here—I got two. You know what a lecture is? It's canned gossip. You want it? Elea, you got it! But first, Joseph, you owe me one. Just what do you say about drugs? About acid?

JOSEPH: I'll tell you what I've heard and what I think. First, before LSD, people didn't believe there was anything to mysticism.

Most thought it a fantasy trip. Well, acid changed all that. Now, we know that if you want to risk it—and I do say risk it—at least do it for the highest reasons and in the best way. That's the sum of the wisdom I've heard. But for me—I'd say technology turns out dream products. The drug trade is the result of chemistry, can't be separated from it. If you have one you will have the other. It's here to stay. People are going to risk it, some for good reasons and others for escape. That's obvious, right? But for me, let me say that there is likely to be a biochemical correlate to every state of mind, so maybe one day we'll be able to match each with each. But, for all that, I suspect that the cost for the perfect enlightenment pill, the most profoundly beautiful *samadhi* wrapped up in a pill or a smoke, will turn escapists into zombies. My best guess is to say that whatever seems good under drugs or alcohol will be better without them.

ELEA: I imagine you have both finished trading position papers, so let's get on with it. Please recall, Harry, that you did turn the discussion over to me, didn't you? I want to return to that last point. Now, Joseph, please don't give another long answer like your last digression; just tell me what would be born from such a pregnancy? If philosophy has something you call philosophical midwifery, shouldn't there be a delivery?

JOSEPH: Most likely, the delivery of an insight into one of those questions we were exploring would be a good birth. And others would be identifying what blocks us from understanding such things and understanding the process that uncovers and removes those blocks.

ELEA: Suppose for a moment that I wanted to explore some of those ideas, especially the one about philosophical midwifery, where would you send me?

JOSEPH: To Plato's dialogues—either the *Theaetetus* or the *Ion* would be a fine beginning. But don't study them alone; work with some friends. We dealt with some of these ideas in our present discussion, but our treatment was shallow compared with Plato's elegance. Take a summer out and see if you can master those dialogues. It is certainly worth it, and you will find the arguments beautifully structured, and like I said, if you decide to do it, you might find it worthwhile to work on it with friends. That's the way I did it.

ELEA: With Harry?

HARRY: Let me ask you a simple question. No tricks, no games this time. If your argument is as good as you think it is, then why is it that I still believe my position? I still believe it's true. Because, don't you see, it seems to me if your argument was really good and sound, I'd be forced to give mine up, wouldn't I? But here it is and it's still intact.

JOSEPH: An argument can't deliver you from your beliefs. An argument is not going to persuade you to abandon a position if you have a need to believe in it. To deliver you from a belief requires an art I don't have. Now, I would love to master the art that delivers men of their false beliefs, and that's why I come here.

ELEA: Would you mind telling us just what you are talking about?

HARRY: Yeah!

JOSEPH: Actually, Sophronicus has the art of philosophical midwifery, and I hope to see a demonstration of it tonight. There are others in this area that practice it, and I hope to master it one day.

ELEA: Sophronicus has this art? Where did he learn it? I've never heard of anyone studying it in college—that's for sure. Why not? I mean, if it's good and it's an art, why not? They teach so much that's not worth learning, so why not teach something that is?

JOSEPH: The wisdom traditions and contemplative arts can't be taught in any of our classrooms. You can lecture on Plotinus' contemplative techniques but not the practice of them. Why? Because universities are designed to expand knowledge in the sciences and social sciences. It's The Doctrine of the Separation of State and

Meaning. You might find it in some kind of Platonic academy, but not in a university. The goal of university education is to inform its students—not to transform them.

HARRY: For once I agree with you. I don't want any "ism" in our institutions and that goes for Marxism, Catholicism, or Platonism. So now it is as clear as can be. The philosopher is transformed into the superior man. The new Jew, the new Superman, and the old justification of tyranny. You've got nothing but another form of elitism. It might work somewhere but it'll never work here. You, of all people, ought to know that. I'll tell you what you've fallen for, Joe—the old messiah game. It's better to have an Archie Bunker-Reagan as our ruler than a philosopher who believes he knows it all. It comes down to who you can trust, those you can understand or those you can't!

JOSEPH: You have the right issue but the wrong politics. The Platonic philosopher only desires to rule himself, not the state.

HARRY: Do I have to tell you about the *Republic*? What else is it but the dictatorship of the philosopher king?

JOSEPH: If you care to reread that work in light of its purpose and its conclusion, you would come to a different conclusion about philosophy and the philosopher.

HARRY: What conclusion?

JOSEPH: In the ninth book of the *Republic*, Socrates says simply and clearly that the state he has been constructing is a contemplative model for the philosopher, and, as such, he has no interest in whether or not it has, or ever will have, a political existence. For the purpose of the *Republic* is to transform the philosopher—not the state.

HARRY: I've heard enough of the *Republic* at SB, but I never heard that one. Why do you believe that?

JOSEPH: It is in the text, Harry, so there is no need to believe it.

HARRY: You know something? I can't believe you're saying that.

In fact, you've become unbelievable! The reason they won't teach this stuff at the university is that it's a pseudo-religion disguised as a philosophy, that's why!

JOSEPH: You may have a good point there too, Harry. I recall that Brehier made the point that Plato's Academy was considered by the state to be a religious institution, but I have no idea what that must have been like during its existence of over a thousand years.

HARRY: More scholarship. That's so much of nothing. You believe knowledge is so damn important, but you know what? Learning is nothing other than imitation. I like the old days before there were schools where men worked as apprentices to learn from others, and these others in turn imitated those before them. Apprenticeship and guilds were the ideal way of insuring that men could appear better because of their superior doing. Schools only came into existence because they needed more men to become doctors, lawyers, captains, etcetera, than the apprenticeship system could handle. Schools were, and still are, second class systems for learning. What we need is the chance to study directly under someone who both appears and is the best. Because imitating through apprenticeship is the superior way of learning, and it produces men who are in every way superior to those clods who have to master their profession through books, notes and study. What makes apprenticeship superior you ask? Well, that is nothing other than the art of imitating.

ELEA: I like that. Not all of it, but it has something in it that I like.

JOSEPH: That's good, Elea.

HARRY: Sure is. It's just as I told you.

JOSEPH: Then, which of you cares to explore it?

HARRY: Just try me. It was my idea.

JOSEPH: Well, you have both agreed it is a good issue and it might be fun to explore but, Harry, do you have the interest to go along?

Will you stay to see where this goes, or will you abandon the ship when you get into trouble?

HARRY: Oh really? That goes for you, too.

ELEA: Sure, that's fair. Go with Harry.

JOSEPH: Then, let me ask you, Harry, do those who imitate learn skills or do they just imitate the shadow of learning called the act?

HARRY: You know what your problem is? You make too much of nothing. I'll tell you what, and I've said it before, you keep making distinctions that don't really matter. You can spin your web of words and bait your hook with distinctions between differences, but for all that, you're not going to catch anything.

JOSEPH: Because?

HARRY: Because it may be fun splitting hairs over these kinds of things, but in the end these distinctions don't really matter, that's why.

JOSEPH: Are you really arguing that differences don't make a difference?

HARRY: And what difference does that make? Just deal with the point—if you can.

JOSEPH: You are right; it shouldn't make any difference, but to explore this issue, Harry, we will have to take a different road than the previous one. But first let me review what I understand to be your position.
          Do you mean that when one has to choose between someone who knows and someone who imitates the one who knows, there is no circumstance or action in which you would prefer the knower over the imitator? Is that right? And, further, are you saying that the difference between these two makes no real difference? Have I grasped your position?

HARRY: Yes, but why make so much of it? All I'm saying is that in most cases—no, in all cases—there isn't any difference that makes a difference between what a knower does and what his imitator does. And just so you don't take my words in their weakest sense I'll make it real simple.Otherwise, you'll strut around here like a peacock believing you've scored another victory when you've really done nothing. Now, when I speak of an imitator I mean the best there is at imitating. And I say that if he hangs around a good surgeon so that he can see all that the surgeon does, so he can watch his every move and attend the surgeon in everything he does—then you and I know that after awhile he will appear like a surgeon and do whatever the surgeon does, and he'll do it perfectly.

And you know what? Then no one can tell whether or not you're knowing or imitating. The superiority of the imitator is that he can do what he does without having to go through all that fuss of getting a medical degree. My conclusion is obvious, isn't it? My imitator would be able to give the perfect appearance of a surgeon, and since he is imitating the best, he will be better at surgery than most surgeons. In fact, he could even appear more confident and secure in what he does than the surgeon himself. Okay, there it is. Now, either deal with my position and not some phoney watered down version of it, or admit that my position is the way things really are, and let's talk about something else.

JOSEPH: You have made a stronger case, and I admire that, but whether or not it is a better case we will have to see. And, Harry, I am glad you are staying in the discussion because I am interested in exploring it.

HARRY: I'm just as interested.

JOSEPH: Now then, as I understand it, you also believe that the perfect imitator, by imitating a perfect surgeon, will perform surgery better than less skilled surgeons; but for all that, you hold, do you not, that it is likely he will not be a better surgeon than the one he imitates—even though he may appear better?

HARRY: You got it right.

JOSEPH: You also say that since the imitator can do all this without having to learn or understand what the surgeon has mastered, he is better off for not having to learn what is unnecessary.

HARRY: That's right on!

JOSEPH: I agree that the good imitator may be able to duplicate the work of a surgeon, but only if the circumstances most closely resembles what he learned to imitate.

HARRY: How's that?

JOSEPH: Well, wouldn't you say that the imitator does his best in circumstances that most closely resemble those he learned to copy or imitate? And, in a similar way, he does his worst work when the circumstances are very different?

HARRY: Yes.

JOSEPH: Then, would you say it is likely that he would prefer to select surgery cases based on those that have the greatest similarities to those he learned to imitate, rather than those with the greatest differences? Or to state the matter simply, he would prefer the same circumstances over different ones, would he not?

HARRY: I would believe so.

JOSEPH: Let me ask you, Harry, does the surgeon encounter patients who are anatomically the same inside and out? I mean, do surgeons become familiar with a wide range of cases where abnormalities among patients is the rule rather than the exception? I don't mean to be complex about this matter, but don't you think the surgeon who has the most surgical experiences will also encounter the most anatomical differences among patients?

HARRY: Perhaps.

JOSEPH: Perhaps? Consider, wouldn't your most excellent of surgeons, the one that your imitator imitates, have vast experience and understand a variety of differences? Wouldn't he have to confront and deal with a variety of anatomical differences among his patient—and by that I mean the different size, shape, and appearance of their organs, nerves, muscles, and bone structures? And, further, must he not also deal with the way these parts function and interrelate with one another and how they vary from patient to patient?

HARRY: Yes.

JOSEPH: Again, would you say that the surgeon would be better able to detect the significance of these differences he encounters among his cases, both when they appear significant and insignificant, or would you say the imitator would?

HARRY: The surgeon would.

JOSEPH: And would the same be true in making diagnoses and recommendations for post operative care? For surely, in these areas of his practice the surgeon also confronts differences, does he not? And, further, must the surgeon determine the significance of such differences when he decides on what he must say and do? Equally, must his skill extend to those times when he decides against surgery and does nothing because he thinks it better?

HARRY: No, not really, because if he did nothing he wouldn't be a surgeon.

JOSEPH: But wouldn't there be times when he reviews all his data on some patient and chooses not to operate? Isn't he functioning as a surgeon when he makes such a judgment?

HARRY: I guess so.

JOSEPH: And when he chooses not to perform surgery in a particular case isn't he deciding that this case differs from those others that require surgery, so that here, too, he confronts difference?

HARRY: Yes, you could say that too.

JOSEPH: Then do you agree with me when I say that knowing the significance of such differences allows the surgeon to apply his skills in the widest range of cases both when he performs surgery and when he decides not to?

HARRY: Yes.

JOSEPH: Tell me, Harry, will the imitator know when to imitate
the surgeon if he decides not to operate? And, if so, just what would
he be imitating? Would he be imitating by doing nothing?

HARRY: No! The imitator would only imitate the surgeon's actions, not when he wasn't active. Obviously he couldn't imitate
nothing. You know when nothing is going on.

JOSEPH: Well then, wouldn't you agree that, on the one hand, the
success of the surgeon depends upon his ability to appreciate, understand, and act upon the differences he encounters in his practice; and that, on the other hand, it must include those times when
his medical judgments include not only deciding on the need to
operate but also whether or not to send his patient to another spe-
cialist?

HARRY: Sure. I guess that follows if you are bound to the logic of
it.

JOSEPH: By contrast, wouldn't you agree that those whose success depends upon their ability to do and say the same thing in the
same way to all alike are only able to imitate the smallest part of
what the knower knows? Further, must we not add that he doesn't
know when it is appropriate to do the same that he does so well?

HARRY: Yes, is that the answer you want?

JOSEPH: Only the answer that seems to follow, Harry.

HARRY: So where does this get us?

JOSEPH: Well, we've reached the conclusion that the imitator ig-
nores differences because they play no role in his imitation, and
he doesn't understand how to deal with such differences because
his only interest is to give the appearance of knowing while he
really knows nothing of what he does.

HARRY: Well, that is an imitator, isn't it?

JOSEPH: And to whom does he appear most successful—to surgeons or those ignorant of medicine?

HARRY: You know the answer to that one.

JOSEPH: Then can't we conclude that difference stands to understanding as sameness stands to appearance and imitation?

HARRY: Seems very simplistic.

JOSEPH: Well, that may be, but are there any weaknesses in what we have been developing?

HARRY: I'm not sure. Maybe so, maybe not.

ELEA: Let me try. I see another side to it, Joseph.

JOSEPH: Sure, go right ahead.

ELEA: The knower does appreciate differences, but differences from what, Joseph?

JOSEPH: From what? Oh, from what should be.

ELEA: And is what should be a model?

JOSEPH: Yes.

ELEA: And being a model, or standard, it would always be the same, wouldn't it?

JOSEPH: Yes.

ELEA: So the knower combines both sameness and difference, doesn't he?

JOSEPH: I see where you are going. He must not only know the significance of the model but the significance of any deviation from the model!

ELEA: Very true.

JOSEPH: Good! Now we can add that to our analogy. We can say that the knowledge of the surgeon combines both sameness—in its use of model—and difference in understanding the significance of any departure from that model, while the imitator lacks both of these and copies only the sameness that exists among particulars.

ELEA: One lives with the higher, the other lives with the lower.

JOSEPH: Yes, one participates in and through models, and so reaches understanding, while the other only copies shadows.

ELEA: True.

JOSEPH: And can't we say the same for all branches of knowledge? For to the degree that they utilize models and such standards to base their judgments on, to predict and anticipate the future, we can say they are systems of knowledge. Surely, that also includes the lawyer and captain, doesn't it?

ELEA: It must.

JOSEPH: Then we have set out what was required?

ELEA: Yes, and that was fun, thanks.

JOSEPH: Yes, that was very helpful. Now, Harry, we should return to your original points. Do you still maintain that the differences between the surgeon and his imitator do not make any difference? Are you still holding that there is no circumstance or action in which you would prefer the knower over the imitator? For we have pointed out that when diagnosis and treatment are required there is no need for the imitator, nor when the surgeon's knowledge and understanding are required is there a need for the imitator, so when would you say the superiority of the imitator becomes apparent?

HARRY: So you got your conclusion, but just look at it—Elea here had to help you conclude. You couldn't do it for yourself, could you? So don't claim any victory and go off tooting your horn.

JOSEPH: You are correct again, Harry. Elea did help. She reminded me of the importance of sameness on a higher level. I may, at times, appear interested in a victory over you, Harry, but I believe that's because in my enthusiasm in pursuing a point I might ignore the human dimension of the dialogue, but that is not the way I would like it to be. I've noticed that I proceed too logically and move far faster than necessary. Maybe I'm a little too argumentative; I'm sure that it makes me look like I'm out to score a victory. I do hope I'll get an insight into why I do that.

ELEA: What's this? Am I some second class citizen around here? Do you mean that if I help develop a point in this discussion it can be minimized if it doesn't help you in your struggle with Joseph? I found it fun, more fun than I've had for quite awhile.

HARRY: And what's that supposed to mean?

ELEA: I might tell you about it later, but this discussion has been good for me. I haven't been able to put into words this issue of imitation and knowledge before. But now, I think I see something. It's the question of what passes for knowledge! Look here, I'll tell you what! Science and everything in that bag is imitation. It really is. Don't they study the processes of nature and put what they find in symbols so that the whole of it mirrors nature? What's that? It's imitating nature, that's what. The mess we're in is because we call that knowledge. So there really isn't any knowledge in science since it is all imitation.

JOSEPH: But do they merely model nature and then imitate it? Don't they adapt it, alter it, and try their best to anticipate the very changes they introduce? And if they do that, are they not understanding what they model?

ELEA: Maybe that's understanding for you, but not for me. They either can't anticipate the effects of what they change or they don't give a damn. Ecological disasters are all over the place because they can't control what they make. And I just don't like thinking that knowledge is something that is out of control. If that's what it is, then we ought to go for wisdom and use science when there is some need to turn and twist something for a good purpose and only when that purpose is good.

JOSEPH: I think you may have a good point-

HARRY: I'm not sure I follow this business of mirroring nature, Elea.

ELEA: In the study of chemistry or physics, for example, what they do is to control the situation so that they can isolate what they want to study, and then they can represent their findings in some mathematical model. In that way you can look at each part of something and see how it relates to the whole. When you can make predictions using that model, then it is adequate. You can then vary this or that and see if it fits expectations based on that model. It's a kind of nuts and bolts approach to nature. They try to figure out the way something is put together—it's like tinker toys. The plans are actually the model you create, and that's nothing but an imitation of the thing. It even looks like the thing. But in chemistry and physics they imitate processes you don't actually see. Still in all, it works the same way.

HARRY: You know, that's a good way to look at it. You map out a picture and you adapt it the way you want. The tinker toy example is good.

JOSEPH: But don't lose sight of the fact that understanding and experimentation both play roles in building that design.

HARRY: So there is no knowledge—just understanding and manipulating imitations. What do you know, I win!

JOSEPH: Only if you appreciate the role of understanding.

HARRY: And if you appreciate the role of imitation.

ELEA: And I don't call that understanding!

HARRY: Why not?

ELEA: Unless you know what the tinker toy is made of, you are only playing games. What is this stuff out of which all this is made? Like, what is it? What would be similar to the wood in the tinker toy example? I wonder if we will ever know. Harry, if we can't get to that—what do we really have? We are born into all this and don't know what it really is. Some people tell me you can't answer that kind of question. If they are right, what can you say you know? It's strange. So, I don't care if science finds newer and smaller parts of parts or parts of wholes. I want to know, what is this stuff?

HARRY: Yeah, you're weird. You forget one thing, Elea—science can tell us how the smallest particles function. That's what they are after. They want to run it all down. Find the smallest stuff out of which all this is made.

ELEA: Didn't I tell you I don't like being called weird? And I'm not the least bit interested in how the parts behave or how they function. All I want to know is– What is it that is functioning that way? If they can't explain that, then you tell me what this is all about.

HARRY: Okay, so maybe you're not weird.

JOSEPH: You have the right questions, Elea, and I like the way you hold onto the ball.

ELEA: Thanks. Anyway, I sure enjoyed the chance of getting into this. It's a good game.

JOSEPH: Yes, it is a higher kind of fun, and it is clear you have a good mind for it. Did you know that play is called the highest activity consecrated to the gods?

ELEA: No, I didn't, but do you mean to tell me that you believe that gods, if they exist, care whether or not we play?

JOSEPH: Elea, you sure caught me on that one because I really don't know how to answer that. It's a fine idea to explore sometime, but not with me. Some people you may know are into it, and they have been holding some seminars on things like Hans Huizianga's *Homo Ludens*.

ELEA: Harry, I was thinking about something when you and Joseph were talking. Do you see yourself as protecting the right to convince others—a kind of amendment to the Bill of Rights?

HARRY: That's a phoney question, or haven't you heard of free speech? Look, if a doctor, lawyer, Indian chief, or anyone else couldn't convince others of the truth of their advice, they would soon go broke. Maybe I didn't do as well as I should have done in this talk, but I got caught with the wrong example and couldn't get out of it. Why I stuck with the surgeon example, I don't know— but once I take a position I go down with the ship, even if it's not my ship. Actually, now that I think of it, my dad does that a lot. We used to argue a lot, only I always lost. Anyway, my point is—what I mean is—that the best money goes to the convincers, and that's as true today as it was yesterday and will be tomorrow.

ELEA: About this convincing, would you say that convincers can convince others whether or not they really know the truth about what they are saying? And do they care whether or not they truly benefit or harm those whom they convince?

HARRY: That was clever. You must have been dreaming that up for awhile.

ELEA: I just wanted to know if those you are convincing assume that you know when they are being convinced?

HARRY: Obviously.

ELEA: You know, don't you, that when you appear as the knower, they don't know you don't know because you conceal that fact from them, and I suspect you must benefit by that deception.

HARRY: A little strong on the language, but it happens everyday.

ELEA: Then, your imitator, in all the disguises he can wear, takes advantage of those more ignorant than himself, and, by doing so, he seeks his own benefit?

HARRY: Why do you make it sound like a morality play? You're trying to convince me of something, too, you know. That's love, too; each cons the other for their own benefit. It's a kind of civilized jungle game; we can't take what we want by force any longer, so today's warriors use words.

ELEA: I guess it's enough that you see my point, Harry. But,

Joseph, is this talk we are having a game like Huizianga says? I'm not sure what I would have to do to make it into something that could be consecrated to the gods. Do you?

JOSEPH: For me? These dialogues test my approach to ideas; it makes me respect them, and I guess that is learning to honor the logos.

ELEA: I knew someone who told me to love as if I were a goddess. It sure sounded great until I realized that for my lover to play his part he would have to be a god himself. Well, rhetoric covers all deception, doesn't it? Is philosophy just like what Huizianga says or is it rhetoric?

JOSEPH: Elea, there is a lot more to philosophy than what I say and do.

ELEA: Such as?

JOSEPH: Well, I'm a beginner at the game. Why don't you tell me about what we've gone through. All I can say is that I do my best at what I do. It's your part to tell me what you see, and after all the talk maybe I can do better later.

ELEA: Well, there is something you said that I can't go along with. You say that Platonic thought is a kind of map or a model to follow. Let's say you follow it, but then, aren't you just modeling yourself to fit something that you admire and look up to? Like here, suppose you succeed, what do you have? You made yourself fit a model, that's all. You actually are only imitating because you train yourself to be like someone else, right? Is that all there is to us? Clay to be modeled this way and that? But what's the clay? Does this make any sense to you?

JOSEPH: You have an interesting way of expressing the problem of the Self.

ELEA: It is not that I don't admire what you have done with yourself. I knew you when, as they say. I like the change, but is all this dialoguing, reading Plato, and stuff—any more than a game?

I'm not saying it's not good to challenge phoney beliefs and get rid of them, but have you, Joseph, ever seen it work on real questions?

JOSEPH: Real questions, means what?

ELEA: Life and death issues, you know—basic stuff. Like, what does all this mean? Have you ever heard a good answer to why you are here? Now, please don't play games with me. Have you found any good answers? I've seen you have the knack for asking questions, but do you have answers, too?

JOSEPH: Well, I've heard ideas such as the soul is immortal, that it survives death and is reborn, reincarnation, and about the soul's journey but–

HARRY: By God, you got him. He's dodging!

ELEA: Wait a minute, I'm not dueling. I want an answer that makes sense right here and now, and I don't care if it's from heaven or hell or Plato—but its got to make sense not in some next world, but right here. The answer has to make sense to me, here, and its got to include why we are talking right here and it's got to make sense now. So forget about heaven, hell, and reincarnation—because they don't answer that problem.

JOSEPH: Of course it does! Your life is your karma. Your present moment of existence is the result of all your present and past thoughts, feelings, and deeds. They live on and fix your future and your future life. Enlightenment burns up your bad karma and makes your next reincarnation better, or it may even, if it is deep enough, take you off the wheel of birth and death altogether!

ELEA: Deep enough? That, dear Joseph, is the problem! Because I know someone who was told that if she didn't continue with her practice, her experience of enlightenment wouldn't have any effect upon her everyday life and that she might, later, even forget it.

HARRY: Would I happen to know her?

ELEA: Yes, you know her. It's my niece, Amy.

HARRY: Well, Amy Nadine is the one to do it all.

ELEA: Enlightenment doesn't make any angels, and you ought to know that as well as me! It is through Amy that I've gotten to know several of these enlightened guys, and it just doesn't wipe out all their bad karma. It's the other way around! It really shows that their karma is stronger than their enlightenment. Maybe that is true for everyone. I don't know. Anyway, why assume it will act in the next world if it doesn't do a good job on this moment that you're in?

HARRY: You got him again!

JOSEPH: And that is interesting, isn't it? You have a good way of expressing yourself. Well, understanding has helped me. I have been able to overcome some of my problems, at least to some degree, and it was through understanding that I gained a real nice insight into the origins of a particular game I had been playing out in my life.

ELEA: I would like to hear about that; I really would because I'd love to know what you are talking about. But you know what I just thought of? That means understanding is stronger than karma and likely to be more permanent and deeper than some of the enlightenment experiences I have heard about. I have even heard that some enlightenment experiences can be so shallow as to have little effect on one's own life. It can even be forgotten, unless one continues the practice of meditation and stuff.

HARRY: Wouldn't it be a gas if your next reincarnation plays itself out only in terms of what you understand about yourself? Because the odds are that neither understanding nor enlightenment will ever get you very far.

JOSEPH: Now, wait a minute. Let's go back to the point Elea was making. Just state what you call the problem once more for me, please.

ELEA: Existence, plain existence, the problem of my being here at this very moment, that's what. And why you are here as well.

JOSEPH: And why do you call that a problem?

ELEA: Now am I right or wrong about this? I've never heard nor read any satisfactory explanation for why I'm here, you know, me—personally—nor have I heard why I'm here rather than somewhere else at some other time. Now, Harry, don't tell me God put me here because that doesn't answer why.

So God may know—but why can't I? I just can't figure out why I can't get a simple answer to a simple question. Now, to me it is obvious that if you can't answer that, then whatever you can answer can't be as interesting as what you can't answer. I guess that bugs me the most. It's strange to be in a place and not know why you're here. Right? Now, I think Harry and I have the same question. Only he ducks it by jumping into belief—but I can't duck it, so I'm stuck with it.

HARRY: Well, dear Elea, that's what faith is for. It ends that! And that's all it has to end. So, Joseph, I do believe it's your time to turn over the discussion to me, isn't it?

JOSEPH: Oh stop crowing, Harry. Sure, Elea's got a good one. And I'm not sure what that means, but I don't know how to answer her.

ELEA: I don't mean to be rude, Joseph, really—and I suspect that what you have learned may have helped you. I can see that, but I'm not sure it will work for me. You see, your answers don't cover me. Are the answers you've heard answering your own questions? Like, do you still have questions like mine?

JOSEPH: Well, I have them now!

ELEA: Rather disturbing isn't it?

JOSEPH: Yes.

ELEA: Maybe you're studying the wrong questions.

JOSEPH: I hear you.

HARRY: Is Elea right? Does your philosophy simply avoid the kinds of questions Elea has? Can you answer her from the Platonic basket of answers, or do you only have questions?

JOSEPH: But I believe—or maybe hope is a better word for it—that there must be an answer to this. It's got to be there. Only right now I have to admit I haven't the faintest idea of where to look for it. It's got to be there—I just don't have it.

HARRY: Hold it! Elea, it's my turn. So, Joseph, you do have a belief, don't you? Ha! Or maybe a prejudice—and you sure could use some help right now, couldn't you? But your friend Sophronicus, or whatever his name is, isn't around so you have to stand on your own, eh?

JOSEPH: Well, you're right there, Harry, more than you know. Elea here is raising the whole issue of what it is to be enlightened or wise, and for me, I really don't know if it covers that.

ELEA: I've heard talk about enlightenment, read a little about it. These pure states of consciousness sound good and maybe I'm strange, but I think, or maybe I believe, or maybe I know that if I were enlightened—and couldn't answer these questions of mine—I wouldn't think too highly of it. I'm not saying it wouldn't be great to be enlightened, but I want to be enlightened about these questions. I really don't think the enlightened have the question, much less the answer.

JOSEPH: Elea, I do believe you could even confound the saints!

HARRY: Invoking the saints! At least I know I don't know and believe—but you–

JOSEPH: Invoking saints I don't even believe in? It was only a figure of speech, that's all. But for me, I think I have to say *I don't know,* and I don't like not knowing, and hope to know. I'm going to push these questions. Thanks for them. I'm really interested in finding if there are answers to them in some tradition, and I sure hope it's in the Platonic tradition.

ELEA: I hope you'll be successful and can find time to share your findings with us. Combining understanding and enlightenment would be quite a trip!

JOSEPH: Yes, it would. I wonder if it's possible—do you think that's what Plato found in Socrates?

HARRY: Have I just been counted out, or something?

JOSEPH: Say, Elea, do you have any other puzzle you play with and can share with me?

HARRY: She's got one that she has been keeping to herself, Joseph. It's wild. She pulled it on me while we were driving over here.

ELEA: I've been puzzled about something. I wonder why I can't recognize everything as mind since I experience everything in my mind. I get an answer to it, and that seems to put it to sleep for awhile. Only it returns with greater force when I see the answer as stupid.

HARRY: See what I mean? She tried it out on me. It's nothing but a logical paradox. There's nothing to it.

JOSEPH: If everything you experience is in your mind, you want to know why you can't recognize that it is in your mind, right?

ELEA: Nope. Why can't I recognize it is all mind? If it's in my mind, it's got to be mind stuff—and if it's seen by the mind, why can't I recognize the whole thing as mind?

JOSEPH: It must be because you believe mind is something else, I think.

ELEA: You're stuck?

JOSEPH: Yes, again. I don't like my answer; it seems hollow.

ELEA: Mine too.

HARRY: Then we all agree on something! What do you know?

JOSEPH: Well it looks like you'll have to excuse me, I see Sophronicus. There are a few things I want to talk to him about before some other people come and get him into a talk.

HARRY: What's the talk going to be on?

ELEA: Yeah, we may owe him coffee. So what's he going to talk about?

JOSEPH: He has been talking about the kind of understanding that philosophical midwifery brings about. I think Sophronicus wants to counter the idea that understanding is like a bunch of roses, or like a friendly fireside chat over coffee. He has been saying that understanding is really threatening and disruptive to many. The quest for understanding the Self, he argues, surfaces a distrust of the process of philosophical midwifery because it awakens the dreaded sense of the unknown and brings us face to face with the fear of losing control since none of us welcomes fundamental changes in our lives. From what I have heard he is going to continue this theme for awhile because there are some of us that want him to discuss how to manage this crisis.

HARRY: There's a guy who warns against a disease he spreads! What's he going to do, call those who disagree with him nuts? We'll have another phoney term like homophobia, won't we? What will he call us? What name will he make up?

ELEA: Oh, I know what I'd call it! Cogniphobia! It is the fear of knowing. I'd like to think he may be right. Say, Joseph, how far do you think understanding can reach? Could it become our own brand of yoga or shamanism?

HARRY: The height of the absurd is when the impotent believe they are pregnant!

JOSEPH: I've wondered about that, too. I don't know. As I said, I have to go. As for our talk, I think we only opened up the discussion on these things. If you two are around again and care to go over this, we can take another look at it.

It was good seeing you again, Harry, and you too, Elea. Maybe

I can hear of your travels another time, Harry.

ELEA: Well, I'll look forward to going back into it. Thanks for the exchange. Harry, do you want to meet again and go into this further?

HARRY: I'll have to give it some thought—maybe. Joseph, see you around. Say, Elea, wouldn't you say that Joseph is walking off and ducking out of a real problem? I think maybe you threw him a bone he can chomp on. Well, have you had enough? Seen enough? Are you ready to leave now?

ELEA: No, Harry, I'm not anxious to leave. I think I'm going to stay around here for awhile and have a cappuccino, not coffee. Care to join me?

HARRY: No. I'll be going along. See you around—maybe.

[CURTAIN]

ANALOGY

THE STRUCTURE OF ANALOGY
DEFINITIONS

In the archetypal analogy there are four *terms*, four *places*, two *ratios*, and three *relations*. The places are where you put the terms. The terms are in *sets*, or *ratios*. The capital letters in the analogy below represent the terms.

ANALOGY:	A	*is to*	B	*as*	C	*is to*	D
PLACES:	lst		2nd		3rd		4th
SETS or RATIOS:	(A	:	B)	as	(C	:	D)

There are three *relations* which are expressed by the words *is to* and *as*. The *is to* relates to the relation of the terms of each ratio while the *as* relates the relations of the ratios.

By substituting a colon (:) for *is to*, and a double colon (::) for *as*, the analogy can be represented or expressed like this:

ratio (A : B) :: (C : D) ratio

Analogies have three kinds of *terms*, they are 1) *numbers* or *lines*; 2) *symbols*; and 3) *ideas*. When terms are *numbers in ratios*, they are called *proportions*.

The first two terms (A : B) are called the *antecedent ratio* and the last two (C : D) are called the *subsequent ratio*. Since analogies are often used to explore the unknown through the known (or the more known) the antecedent ratio expresses known and the subsequent relation the unknown.   more known :: unknown

There are three *relations* in a four place analogy; the relations between the terms (2), and the relation between the ratios (1).

Analogies are used to 95
explore the unknown through the known.

This four term archetypal analogy can be transformed in two ways—
either by taking the terms *conversely,* reversing the order of the terms
in each ratio/set; or by inverting the terms, that is by taking the first
and third terms together to form the antecedent ratio and the second
and fourth together for the subsequent ratio. By using these two ways
of transforming the analogy we can generate the eight forms of the
archetypal analogy.

Listed here are eight transformations and the classic names of the
first four analogies:

VERSE	(1)	A : B	::	C : D
CONVERSE	(2)	B : A	::	D : C
INVERTENDO	(3)	A : C	::	B : D
CONVERSE of the INVERTENDO	(4)	C : A	::	D : B
INVERTENDO of the CONVERSE	(5)	B : D	::	A : C
	(6)	D : B	::	C : A
	(7)	C : D	::	A : B
	(8)	D : C	::	B : A

These eight transformations are the major transformations of the archetypal analogy. But you might want to discover if there are others;
however, restrict yourself to simple transformations, those based on
non-combinations of terms.

Notice the sequence of these transformations as it proceeds through
these transformations. First the transformation begins *within* the ratio
A:B and becomes B:A as C:D becomes D:C. Then the changes occur
between the terms of the ratio as A:C and B:D.

Through these eight transformations the terms of this type of analogy
are distributed in a variety of ways but the position of the first ratios,
which is called the antecedent ratio, and the second, the subsequent
ratio, of course, remains fixed. Notice that the order of the terms in
the first ratio (antecedent) repeats itself in the second ratio (subsequent ratio) forming an ordered pair.

After reviewing how analogies undergo transformations, consider that in understanding the construction of the terms of the first ratio it is simple to determine the terms of the last ratio.

As you review the following terms of the antecedent ratio, please consider what would be the terms of the subsequent ratio:

A : C :: _____ : _____
D : C :: _____ : _____
D : B :: _____ : _____
B : A :: _____ : _____

Substitute ideas for the symbols to determine for yourself if the meaning of the analogy remains the same when the positions of the terms within the analogy change.

As the Shepherd is to his Sheep, so too the Ruler is to his Subjects.

Note the verse form below:

VERSE   **Shepherd : Sheep :: Ruler : Subjects**

For practice, make the following transformations using the terms from the above analogy:

CONVERSE *Sheep* : *shep* :: *subj* : *ruler*

INVERTENDO *shep* : *ruler* :: *sheep* : *subj*

CONV. INVERTENDO *ruler* : *shep* :: *sub* : *sheep*

Now after considering the following ways of relating the terms, see if these have the same kind of meaning as those above.

Shepherd : Subjects :: Sheep : Rulers
Rulers : Sheep :: Subjects : Shepherd
Subjects : Sheep :: Rulers : Shepherds

What meaning would there be to say a shepherd relates to subjects?

[handwritten: In Analogy, the relationships are similar, not the same, and one is used to help explain the other]

Or that sheep relate to rulers?

Is the relation between the shepherd and his sheep exactly the same as
  the relation between the ruler and his subjects?

[handwritten: relationship is not exactly the same.]

How would you describe the difference between the ideas of same,
  similar, and identical?

Does the ruler take his subjects to the high meadows to feed on grass?

Is the relation between the shepherd and his sheep also similar to the
  relation between a teacher and his students?

Or a doctor and his patients?

And between a captain and his crew? To what common class do all
  these pairs belong? *[handwritten: They are the stronger, knowledgible function is to help the weak]*

A Shepherd is to his Sheep	as	A Ruler is to his Subjects
?		guides
? *[handwritten: knowledge]*		protects
?		rules
?		feeds

[handwritten: knowledge for the purpose of benefit]

If you continue this list and specify all the ways you can describe the
relations between the terms in each ratio you will discover something
interesting. Not all the relations of the one can be found in the other.

Are there always some relations that cannot be transferred to the other
  ratio? *[handwritten: Yes.]*

Or would you say shearing and feeding function in both ratios? Is the
way a shepherd relates to his sheep the *same* or *similar* to the way a
teacher relates to his students? Or the way a doctor is to his patients?

Can you think of other sets of terms that are similar? What does it
mean to say there is a relationship that is common to all these cases,
or ratios? *[handwritten: That the terms within the ratios share similar functions + properties to that subsequent to them]*

For if the way a physician relates to his patients is the *same* as the way a captain does to his crew, then the physician would be right in demanding his patients do exactly as he tells them or he could charge them with mutiny!

So the physician relates, *not* in the *same* way, but in a *similar* way as the captain to his crew. So that while we can say that a physician charts his patients' journey to health we know it is not in the same way a captain charts his journey.

However, both the physician and the captain have to anticipate the future for those who seek the benefit of their respective art.

the weaker seek the benefit of the stronger

THE SQUARE OF ANALOGY

To test for the validity of any four-term analogy you can use the Square of Analogy. Place the antecedent terms along the top of the square and the subsequent terms along the bottom, as indicated in the figure.

parallel lines moving in the SAME DIRECTION

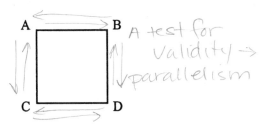

A test for validity → parallelism

Valid analogies are formed by parallel lines moving in the same direction on the square. Hence, all analogies formed by lines that are not parallel and/or not moving in the same direction are not valid. *Test the rule yourself* by forming both valid and invalid analogies from the square. See if you can determine whether or not these analogies make sense. Examine the analogy:

Shepherd *is to* **:** **Sheep** *as* **::** **Ruler** *is to* **:** **Subjects**

and compare it with the analogy:

Sheep   :   Rulers   ::   Subjects   :   Shepherds

When the number of terms in an analogy is expanded we have a more complex analogy. A series of analogies can be constructed with terms that are parallel. The result of this kind of construction is called the *matrix of analogy,* and, as you will see, it is an instrument for comparing what is known with what is unknown. Accordingly, we place the known ratio first and the unknown second. The antecedent ratio, being the known ratio, is what we are more familiar with while the consequent ratio, the unknown, is not totally unknown but rather is what we find puzzling or mysterious. Consider: What presents man with more problems, the way mankind has cared for sheep or the way man is cared for by his rulers? Are not the issues of how to rule, who should be entrusted with ruling, and what are the rights of rulers against the rights of subjects among the most perplexing problems?

What might we learn by studying the different ways men rule—anything? Could we structure this issue analogically?

Let's try. Consider the following ratio:

A Shepherd : his Sheep

Now expand it to:

A Shepherd : his Dog : his Tent : his Knowledge : his Sheep

and contrast it with these parallel terms:

A Ruler : his Army : his Castle : his Knowledge : his Subjects

Now, do the same with the following:

Captain :	_____ :	_ship_ :	_____ :	**his Crew**
Physician :	_nurses_ :	_office_ :	_____ :	**his Patients**
Teacher :	_____ :	_school_ :	_____ :	**his Students.**

(handwritten: Arts)

(handwritten at bottom: different in how their knowledge benefits subjects)

Is the knowledge the same in each of these arts? Does one kind of art differ from another not only in the benefit the subject receives but also in terms of the depth of knowledge the ruler must possess?

If so, can you rank the arts, hierarchically that is, in terms of the degree of knowledge required to rule effectively? What art would be named that would be at the top of the list?

THE MEAN ANALOGY   3 terms*

The mean analogy is the most aesthetically pleasing for it naturally has a higher degree of simplicity, harmony, symmetry and order than other forms of analogy. Interestingly, some philosophers use the mean analogy as their special tool to explore metaphysics and theories of cosmology.

simplicity
harmony
symmetry
order

Can you make an analogy from the following statement?

"God made man in his own image and likeness."

extremes

The mean analogy has only three terms:

means

VERSE (1)	A :	B ::	B	: C
CONVERSE (2)	B :	A ::	C	: B
INVERTENDO (3)	B :	C ::	A	: B
CONVERSE of the INVERTENDO (4)	C :	B ::	B	: A

As you can see, the invertendo analogy is taken from the converse and not from the verse form because when you generate the invertendo from the verse you don't get a new analogy, you get the verse. Explore it yourself. Try making different combinations to see if you can generate a new form of the mean analogy.

Compare the archetypal analogy with the mean analogy; notice that the mean analogy accomplishes in four transformations, four steps, what the four term analogy takes eight steps to do: all terms in all places. Notice that in these four forms of the mean analogy there are eight ratios of two terms and within these combinations are expressed all possible simple combinations of the mean analogy.

Consider the four forms of the mean analogy: if you draw a line through all the A terms, all the C terms, connect the B terms together in a circle, note how the antecedent ratio and its converse moves to the subsequent position just as the subsequent moves to the antecedent position, and also note that the extreme and mean terms exchange positions.

Does this indicate a high degree of order, balance, and harmony of terms within the mean analogy?

Does the four term analogy have the same possibilities?

SIMILES AND METAPHORS

To generate *similes* and *metaphors* from an archetypal analogy you need only follow a basic generating principle: use any invertendo ratio and substitute *like* to produce a simile, and *is* or *are* to produce a metaphor. Using this principle and the above analogy of the shepherd, we can generate the simile *a shepherd is like a ruler,* and the metaphor would be *subjects are sheep.* When an author you are reading uses a simile or metaphor, you can work backwards and discover the analogy that is guiding his thought. Consider, the following analogy:

Shepherd   :   Sheep   ::   Ruler   :   Subjects

Which of the following are similes and which are metaphors?

- A shepherd is like a ruler.
- Subjects of a state often act as if they were sheep.
- A ruler is a shepherd.
- Subjects are sheep and should be treated as such.

Now that we have dealt with the issue of generating similes and metaphors, let us reflect on the condition that made it possible:

The ratio *shepherd: sheep* and *ruler: subjects* both belong to the same class, do they not? Consider, in both of them one of the terms is a master and the other the subject. Then they both presuppose mastership.

Would you say the other analogies we were making all fit into this one category of mastership?

Now, for another look at the simile and metaphor, notice that we can say:
- a Shepherd *is like* a Doctor
- a Shepherd *is like* a Ruler
- a Shepherd *is like* a Captain

Or we can say:
- a Doctor *is like* a Shepherd
- a Ruler *is like* a Shepherd
- a Captain *is like* a Shepherd

As you examine these two ways of expressing a simile would you say one seems to fit more likely than the other?

Which way has more *accuracy?* If *a shepherd is like a doctor,* would the image that comes to your mind be different than if *a doctor is like a shepherd?*

Given that the standard verse form of the analogy places the known ratio first and the more unknown second, does that suggest that the invertendo relation of A : C is not the same as C : A? And that the ratio proceeding from the unknown to the known is, in most cases, more illuminating about the subject than from the known to the unknown.

Could it be that what we call the unknown ratio contains more than the known?

Consider: Does the ruler require more from himself to rule justly than it does for the shepherd to rule his flock? Does the art of ruling require a greater insight into man and into what it is to be a just ruler than the ruling of sheep by the shepherd?

Thus, the ratios that we include in the class of mastership must share something in common and that is being a ruler, having knowledge of ruling, and subjects to rule. In this simple statement is the whole issue of politics and philosophy:

What kind of knowledge must the ruler have to achieve a just rule? And if someone rules without that knowledge, would you not agree that the name ruler is being misapplied?

How many subjects must a ruler have to be a ruler since there must be subjects? Ten thousand? Ten? One?

A ruler can rule a state, then, with only one subject, himself, and if the ruler rules with mastership he should rule justly.What kind of knowledge must a ruler have to rule justly?

The answer to this question is explored in depth in Plato's *Republic*.

Consider the simile as *Likeness* because it brings together into a unity its extremes. In the analogy:

$$A \ : \ B \ :: \ C \ : \ D$$

there are two pairs of similes—for (A : C) and (C : A) is one pair; (B : D) and (D : B) is the other.

Note that each term has a *similarity* to the other term *in the other ratio* and that *likeness* includes fulfilling a *similar role* or position *in the other ratio*. It is this joining to *similarity* through these relationship-pairs that brings the extreme terms into a unity based upon Likeness.

THE ALLEGORY

To generate an allegory from an archetypal analogy, first take a four term analogy:

Shepherd : Sheep :: Ruler : Subjects

Next, expand the number of terms in the antecedent ratio in a natural order or sequence:

₁) expand antecedent terms

Shepherd : Dog : Tent : Shepherd's Knowledge : Sheep

Then find parallel terms to each of those terms by discovering terms that function in a similar way:

₂) expand subsequent terms in same way.

Ruler : Army : Castle : King's knowledge : Subjects

And, finally, while telling or relating a story in the first set of terms introduce into the story the key or important parts of the second set. Consider the expanded analogy:

Shepherd : Dog : Tent : Shepherd's knowledge : Sheep

::

Ruler : Army : Castle : King's knowledge : Subjects

Thus, an allegory can be set into motion when a challenge or task is given to the characters in the story. An example of this is the Allegory of the Cave in Plato's *Republic* (Book VII). The ignorant or unenlightened can be said to live in a cave (1) as the enlightened live in the upper world (2). The basic analogy is:

Unenlightened : Cave :: Enlightened : Upper World

To expand:

(1) a) The ignorant, who live in the caves, believe the shadows they experience on the wall of the cave to be real.

(1) b) But they are chained in such a way that they are unable to see anything but the shadows.

(2) a) The enlightened live in the upper world experiencing the true reality, the sun, and light and

(2) b) They are free to experience all the things that truly live and exist in the light of reality.

The expanded analogy reads:

Unenlightened : Belief   : Shadows   : Cave

::

Enlightened   : Knowledge : True Beings : Upper World

Using these elements Plato now tells a story, showing how man moves from one world to the other. Our task, as a reader, is to find those philosophical terms, or ideas, that are similar to those in the allegory. If you decide to explore this allegory you will easily discover many more interesting points about the cave-upper world that has equally surprising relationships to the dialogue itself.

When you explore for the identities of the corresponding terms from the allegory you should be able to discuss and explain what the Sun means on the level of philosophy and its meaning for those questing for enlightenment. In the same way all the terms that describe the course of studies of the philosopher have their parallel terms throughout the *Republic,* and the reader is required to do the work to *unpack,* or understand, Plato. When you look for such parallels, you may want to read different translations, since many don't approach their translation from the perspective of its value to those who value retaining in any translation those metaphors and similes that are in the original text. But, how much do translations differ? There are many examples of this translation problem: Check for yourself the way the Greek word, *paideia (παιδείας),* is translated in the Jowett, Rouse, and other translations of the *Republic.*

Note the differences found in two different translations by Rouse and Jowett:

"Next, then I said, take the following parable of education and igno-rance as the picture of the condition of our nature."
[Rouse translation]

"And, now, I said, let me show in a figure how far our nature is en-lightened and unenlightened."
[Jowett translation]

Compare them for their differences. For Rouse, it is a *parable,* but for Jowett he will show in a *figure.* Which term is more accurate? Why?

Notice the key term that describes those in the story; would the terms *educated* and *ignorant* be the same as *enlightened* and *unenlightened?* Imagine the most educated; would that be the most enlightened? Could the most educated be among those unenlightened?

Given the description of those who are enlightened, are the philoso-phers among them? How are philosophers described in the *Republic?* Would a description of them have to include the idea of being *enlight-ened?* Why?

One of the most central puzzles in philosophy is the relationship between *the Good* and *the Idea of the Good;* and to deal seri-ously with this question brings one to Plato's use of analogy. The word *idea* is a word we have *adapted* from the Greek, *it does not mean a thought, a concept, or even an idea.* It is a word that expresses *seeing* and it has the sense of *to behold* or *to see the Good.* Now, what it would mean to *behold the Good* is given in the *Republic as "the most brilliant light of being."* That means, of course, we can say that it refers to the luminosity or radiance that Plato speaks about in several dialogues. One of the high points of the cave-upper-world allegory is an analogy that the reader must work out to discover this relationship between *the Good* and *the Idea of the Good.*

Consider this quote:

*"... in the world of the known, last of all is the idea of the good, and
with what toil to be seen! And seen, this must be inferred to be the
cause of all right and beautiful things for all, which gives birth to
light in the world and the king of light in the world of sight, and, in the
world of mind, herself the queen produces truth and reason; and she
must be seen by one who is to act with reason publicly and privately."*
                                                (Rouse, p. 316).

Look up the complete quote yourself, see how it plays a role in the
allegory, recover the entire paragraph, reflect on the above section
and its construction, and notice that for you to understand it you will
have to work it out for yourself.

What are the different kinds of worlds he describes? Is there a Royal
pair in each world? What would be the King and Queen in each? What
are the implications of this analogy on the *Republic?*

The Allegory of the Cave-Upper World is related to the Divided Line
in Book VI of the *Republic.* In that book Socrates is urged to describe
the *perfect model of the Good* (Rouse, p. 303) and to do that he develops an analogy with the Sun and Light; but Glaucon urges him to go
further and make his meaning about the Sun clearer. Socrates con-
structs his famous Divided Line (a mean analogy), and that, in turn, is
used as the basis for the Allegory of the Cave-Upper World. Now,
here is some work! Approach it with care, take the time necessary and
decipher what Plato has given us because in that unfolding, or *un-
packing,* of the analogies and allegories, we come to the conditions
for understanding.   the second set of terms

A *parable* is an allegory whose key terms are not revealed except to a
select inner circle and, for the inner circle, the parable then becomes
an allegory or analogy. When Jesus tells his disciples why he uses
parables in his teaching ministry, he explains that *"To you has been
given the secret of the kingdom of God, but for those outside everything is in parables."* As Jesus goes on to say, it is so those outside

may hear but not understand, *"lest,"* according to the Gospel of Mark, *"they should turn again and be forgiven."*

The source for this remark is from Isaiah. Do you think you might look it up? Would you be interested in contrasting the two judgements side by side and contrasting them? When you do, will you look into the word *lest*? What does it do in that sentence? What would follow if the truths were to be given freely for everyone's benefit? What is the meaning of fulfilling a prophecy when the actions predicted are arranged to meet the terms of the prediction?

When an allegory is both political and comical it is called a *satire*.

2 X 2 TABLE OF COMPARISON

Consider the following table:

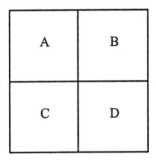

We call this a 2 by 2 table of comparison because, using it as our model, we can compare either by rows, columns, or diagonally:

1) By rows: a is to b; c is to d   (the reverse b is to a; d is to c).
2) By columns: a is to c; b is to d   (the reverse c is to a; d is to b).
3) Along the diagonals:

         a is to d; b is to c   (the reverse d is to a; c is to b).

Consider these twelve ways of relating as exhausting the combinations possible within the 2 by 2 table.

Now, let us take an example from Socrates' Speech on Love found in Plato's *Symposium:*

Teacher	Student
DIOTIMA	SOCRATES
SOCRATES	AGATHON

You can then reflect and compare:
1) The relations between Diotima and Socrates
2) The relations between Socrates and Diotima
3) The relations between Socrates and Agathon
4) The relations between Agathon and Socrates
5) Socrates as student and Socrates as teacher
6) Diotima and Socrates as teachers
7) Socrates and Agathon as students
8) The gap that exists between Diotima and Agathon

Why are there only eight relations shown here instead of the twelve as mentioned previously? Why are diagonals allowed here but were judged as invalid within four term analogies?

Examine the way that Socrates, Agathon, and Diotima are described in the *Symposium.* Reflect on the characters in the myth that Socrates uses to explain the origin of Love—Poverty, Plenty, Aphrodite, and Love.

Can you find similarities between these two sets of characters? What would it *mean* if the characters in the dialogue could be candidates for being similar to the figures in the myth? Can they? What would it mean?

If there are several ways in which these characters in the dialogue and the myth can be similar, are there some differences that eliminate some of these possibilities?

Remember that after Plenty passes out on nectar in Zeus's garden, Poverty seduces him and conceives Love. How could *that* be similar to what takes place in the garden? By the way, did Socrates *pass out* before arriving at the house of Agathon?

If you like puzzles of this kind you are taking on the task of treating Plato's myths as analogies which can provide you with an additional level of meaning for these dialogues. Every myth in Plato has an interesting meaning well worth discovering, and most can fit together into a mosaic that contains the journey of the philosopher.

Before leaving this subject, let me ask: What significance have you discovered in Diotima's remark to Socrates that the children of a philosophical relationship can be said to rival not only the poets, but Homer and Hesiod? What works today would you mention that would be similar to the works of Homer and Hesiod in Socrates' day?

Again, what does it mean if the nature of reality is such that only the mind can see it or encounter it? What would it mean for there to be some relationship between mind and reality? Is beauty an Idea? But is an idea of Beauty merely a thought or concept?

A way of understanding that an Idea in Plato is *not* merely a thought but something to be realized and that only after much reflection can be seen in the Idea of Beauty in the *Symposium*.

What would you be doing if you were to see yourself going up those steps that lead to Beauty? What would be happening to you? Examine how the notion of *bringing to birth* plays itself out in the steps leading to Beauty. Can you find four kinds of *birth?* If you only found three you missed one worth noticing. What culminates the journey to Beauty? What position does the person who ascends those steps finally reach?

Now let us consider the analogy from Book VI of Plato's *Republic:*

Wisdom : Understanding :: Belief : Image thinking
(ignorance)

Please Note: *Understanding* and *Belief* are sufficiently similar because they proceed from things accepted as true but not known to be true. Thus, in this key respect, since they are judged as the same for analogical purposes, they can be contrasted in a mean analogy.

What is the difference between contrasting them in a three and a four term analogy? What is the significance of this point? It is likely to require rereading Book VI of Plato's *Republic.*

From the four term analogy of the *Republic* we now move to the three term analogy in the *Symposium.* (Keep the 2 X 2 Table in mind.) As we previously discussed, this analogy can be transformed in the four ways.

Please review Socrates' speech in the *Symposium* and carefully note the contrasts he makes in the opening paragraph of his recollection of the speech of Diotima. Socrates describes her as his teacher and a Master of the Art of Love. *"She it was who taught me about love,"* says Socrates. Diotima is described in the dialogue as a prophetess, a priestess; and later he describes the way she functions as a philosopher. Some of these contrasts can be structured in terms of the mean analogy:

Wisdom : Right Opinion :: Right Opinion : Ignorance
Diotima :   Socrates   ::   Socrates   :   Agathon

Socrates uses the same process with Agathon as Diotima used with him and this means that Agathon has the opportunity of moving from ignorance to right opinion; but whether he can move higher into the realm beyond opinion, we do not know. Therefore, we can represent these features of the dialogue in an analogical structure that grasps these essentials.

Now, consider, as Diotima, possessing the fullness of philosophy, provides the way for Socrates' development; and he is able to receive it So too, Socrates, becoming full, provides the opportunity for Agathon who struggles to receive as much as he is able. Socrates can now function as a bridge since he can now give what he has received. If the giving continues—that is if Agathon becomes full and can then give also—that giving constitutes a tradition.

When one theme plays itself out and that theme continues being played in a variety of ways over time, this is Harmony—whether it be of the same or a different tradition.

For Socrates' speech on Love and to explore the above progression, please once again read the *Symposium,* in *The Dialogues of Plato,* translated by Rouse, on pages 94 -106.

THE MOLECULAR PROPOSITION

In each case we see the relation between two sets of terms. Each set of terms is called a ratio. We can represent these ratios symbolically. The different relationships can be represented by numbers. There can, of course, be more than three relations for each ratio.

A	Rl	B		C	Rl	D
	R2				R2	
	R3				R3	
	n				n	

significance

This form of analogy is called *the molecular proposition.* The molecular proposition is a <u>symbolic</u> <u>representation</u> of analogy that includes within itself the <u>basic principles</u> of logic, math, and analogy.

THE BASIS OF NATURAL LAW

W̱e can build a set of parallel terms upon the basic analogy when the functions are similar.

Add relations to the ratio:

Shepherd : Sheep

Complete the consequent ratio below:

Shepherd	:	Sheep	::	Ruler	:	Subjects
		1) guides		1)		
		2) protects		2)		
		3) rules		3)		
		4)		4)		
		5)		5)		

Would you say the same relations that you identified above can be used to describe the relations in the following ratios? Why in some and not in others? Create a theory to account for that difference.

knows how to help for ← **Physician** : **Patients**
patient's benefit

	:	
Captain	:	**Crew**
Physician	:	**Patients**
Teacher	:	**Students**
Horseman-trainer	:	**Horses**
Merchant	:	**Customers**
Tennis coach	:	**Tennis players**
Druggist	:	**Customer**
Thief	:	**Gang of thieves**

does not guide, protect ← **Merchant**
knows how to pursuade
for his own benefit

Among these (sets) pairs of terms in the above ratios, would you say they all require knowledge? In what way is the physician's knowledge of medicine different from the knowledge of the merchant? Which of these ratios would you say requires the greater amount of knowledge of the subject?

ANALOGY AS A MODEL FOR ANALYSIS

L et us take the physician as an example and ask what is entailed in his profession so that he can benefit a patient. When someone is ill, or is in pain from some injury, and desires to recover their health they seek out someone who they believe has the knowledge to deal with their condition, that is a *physician*. The physician, after making a medical examination, makes a diagnosis, designs a treatment plan, or a therapy, and monitors the patient to overcome an illness or an injury that his patient has suffered. The accumulated experience and knowledge of the physician develops into an idea of healthiness which, of course, is an ideal and may never be seen in the physician's experience. But without this ideal the physician can not be an effective physician. A medical examination of a patient is the result of reflecting on the ways the patient's condition differs from this idea of healthiness; thus, it is making a comparative judgement. Thus, the purpose of the medical examination is to discover in what way such differences from that ideal indicate some particular illness.

If one physician is better at diagnosing patients than another physician, it is likely that it is because one can better judge this difference between the ideal of healthiness and the patient's condition. Once this difference has been understood and put into words—which we call a diagnosis—then the physician can recommend certain procedures for the patient to follow which we call a *therapy,* or a treatment plan. The diagnosis names the condition (which if allowed to run its course would harm the patient) and the *therapy,* or treatment plan, is designed to either reverse that condition, lessen its effects, or assist the patient through the illness or injury. Whatever plan the physician decides upon is based upon a strategy to close the gap between that ideal of health and what is realizable for his patients. To increase the likelihood of closing the gap between the patient's deficiencies and this ideal, the physician may recommend exercises, medicine, diet, and even suggest changes in the patient's life style.

If the patient is convinced that the physician has the necessary knowledge to help him achieve a better condition, and understands he should follow the treatment plan, then he follows the physician's orders. The patient then, in accepting those instructions, is ruled by the physician, and he, in turn, becomes a subject. It is only because the patient believes that the knowledge the physician possesses may benefit him that he willingly undergoes the treatment plan. For certainly, the patient would not be willing to endure even more pain than that he had previously been experiencing unless he believes that he will be benefited by the course of treatment. Indeed, it is not at all unusual for patients of dentists to undergo more pain in the treatment phase than what was experienced during the illness.

Further, the physician must go beyond merely treating the patient because there is a need to supervise the changes the patient goes through until a full recovery is made because it might be necessary for the physician to vary the treatment plan according to the changes that the patient undergoes. It is because the physician can anticipate the possibility of a range of changes and has learned to adjust his treatment plan that he can be said to understand the course of treatment of his patients; these judgements are, simply, knowledgeable anticipations of what may occur in the future.

The physician can be said to be able to see through his knowledge into the future; his knowledge provides a basis for making a diagnosis and treatment plan. All arts have a capacity to anticipate the future, and it is because of this that they are said to possess a kind of foretelling of the future which can be called a rational prophecy. To anticipate the future through an art was first expressed by the Ancient Greeks in the myth of Prometheus. For he was the god who saved the race of man from extinction by stealing the Arts and Fire from Zeus and presenting them to man as a gift. In the name of the god we see the idea of foretelling because *Prometheus means to see ahead,* or *having forethought.*

Now, let us express what we have been saying in the following way: Diagnosis plays a central role in every art; it is making an analysis and understanding a crisis as a deviation from the ideal; from that difference, or deviation, a procedure, therapy, or treatment plan is devised to intervene and end the crisis by bringing the situation closer to the ideal. Those that accept the terms of the treatment plan become the subject that may benefit from the ruler's practice of that art.

Thus, the one who rules subjects through a knowledge of medicine is a physician, the one that rules subjects through a knowledge of seamanship is a captain, and, in general, those who rule by an art do so through knowledge. The subjects, in turn, accept the commands of their ruler and do so in the belief that they will benefit by following the knowledge of their ruler.

Or to express this in an analogy, we can say:

Diagnosis *is to* discovering the difference between an ideal and the subject's condition *as* therapy *is to* a treatment plan to bring the subject closer to that ideal.

Consider again: under the course of treatment of any art there can be but one goal and that is to benefit the subject of the art. The subject benefits when he is brought closer to the ideal for that art. For each art—in so far as it is an art—has a particular benefit or excellence it can bestow on its subjects. Each art has an ideal, and the practitioner of the art uses the knowledge of the art to close the gap between the condition of the subject and the ideal of the art.

Consider then: Would you say for every ideal of man there should be a corresponding art that could bring man to that excellence or perfection? Then, if man is perfectible, there should be an art that can perfect him; if so, what would be the name of that art? If there is an art of philosophy, what would be its ideal and how would it better its subject?

Now, let us return once again and consider our list of ratios on page 114.

Can you separate those you would call an art from the others? Can you identify those that exist to benefit the subject, but not the practitioner of the skill? Can you identify those that exist primarily to benefit the practitioner? Can you identify those that possess an ideal for the subject from which they can judge the benefits to the subject?

If the merchant can charge whatever he wants for whatever reason, then shouldn't the physician do the same? If the merchant breaks no laws when he raises his prices for his goods and services during times of emergency, shouldn't a physician be allowed to charge more when his patients are in pain than when they are not? Then, wouldn't the best time for a physician to set his fee for his services be when the patient is suffering the most?

Should a captain of a ship be allowed to renegotiate his fees and to charge his passengers more when he finds his passengers are fearful of losing their lives during a heavy storm? What, then, would you say if a physician were to practice medicine as a merchant conducts his business? It is because of this idea of an art or profession that we expect practitioners to be primarily concerned with benefiting their subject instead of themselves.

The Why

For it is when the physician practices his art as a merchant that we charge him with malpractice; and the captain is called a pirate when he puts his own advantage above that of his crew and passengers. This idea of art has existed for centuries and is the basis of many international laws; it is called *natural law.* When people enter into these professions/arts, they *must* benefit the subject or be brought into court and judged as violating the law, a natural law.

Now, what argument would you use to justify bringing all the arts in our list together and on what basis would you exclude others?

Professions, or arts, must benefit the subjects of that art; this is natural law.

Rflections on the "As If"

Now, let us take one of the ideas explored in *Is It All Relative?* such as those found in the New Testament story of the divine luminosity that radiated through Jesus and from which Moses and Elijah emerged and then talked with Jesus. After witnessing this extraordinary event, Peter asked Jesus if he should build three tabernacles, and Jesus responded by saying they should tell no one what they had seen. Now, if this story has a meaning that is well worth considering analogically, then we will have to ask some questions.

How similar is the story of Moses building a tabernacle with that of Jesus? What was meant by the *tabernacle?* Why did Moses set out to build it, and what role did it play in Judaism?

If there is an example of divine luminosity in the Moses story, how similar is it to the Jesus story?

Did Elijah play a major role in Judaism? If so, what role?

What works will you have to read to explore this further? Who might you consult with?

As you reflect on all the miracle stories, would you give this event greater or less significance? Why?

Consider further: Did a mountain play a central role in each story? Why?

What role did Moses and Elijah play in Judaism? What would it mean then for all three to discuss together?

If Peter, after witnessing this event, thought it appropriate to build a tabernacle, what would it mean to build three—one for each? Is there an analogy between these events?

What would it mean then to say that *as* Jesus is to the divine luminosity *so too* Moses was to the divine luminosity? What would it mean to say that Jesus's role is similar to Moses' role as Moses' role is similar to Elijah's role?

If God's presence is carried *by and through* the tabernacle, then what would that mean if three tabernacles were built? Why the secrecy? What is it about this event that Jesus would want kept secret?

Notice, we are creating a series of questions and setting up analogies to explore our findings. This is the way you can learn to speculate. Try it! And good luck!

MORE REFLECTIONS ON ANALOGY

Reflecting on analogy brings you to a new kind of thinking. It is like finding a strange doorway that if you can pass through it you will find it opens into a land that has its own kind of wonder. The door is the idea of sets or classes. Consider, there are various sets of ideas we might explore; for example, we might study the idea of *Time*, and if we did so we would explore the members of that set, or class, and that would include the present, past and future time. But since our concern is with analogy we will explore the set of ideas used to understand analogy not only because these ideas form the vocabulary necessary for understanding analogy but because these same ideas are essential for the reflecting on the nature of reality. This way of reflecting and exploring ideas does not depend upon science or the data of the senses but only what can be understood in and through the use of reason alone—it is this kind of study that is called metaphysics.

The fundamental ideas of metaphysics are One and Many, and from each of these ideas it is possible to derive others as if they were pearls strung together on a single strand which we can call a class-string. Thus, we can speak of the One as the string, or set, having members such as *oneness, identical, same, similar,* and like; equally we can say that there is another string called the class of Many, having members such as *manyness, different, other, dissimilar,* and *unlike.* Clearly, the set of One and Many are opposites and so too are its corresponding members. While these terms will help us study analogy they can serve as a bridge for the study into metaphysics. So let us use these terms to explore analogy and then pass into the domain of metaphysics. But first let us reflect on a few things that you will find obvious:

If two things are exactly the *same* in all respects, would they still be two things? Or would they be *identical?* And, if identical in all respects, would they not be one?

Then, if there are *things* in the universe, must they not be *different* from some *other* things? Otherwise there wouldn't be *many* things, would there? There would only be *one.*

Then, if there are *things* in the universe, there must be some *difference* among them, yet since they are each what we call a thing, they must have some *sameness* to them, or we wouldn't call them all things.

Then, would it not follow that any two things taken at random must have some common feature that distinguishes them from each other and some difference that makes them different?

Since we can put things that share some sameness in the same class, would it not follow that we can find a class for everything in the universe?

Then, we can talk about things and their classes; we can talk about what it is for a thing to be a thing and what it is for a class to be a class, can we not?

Surely, since things and classes can be distinguished in terms of their sameness, does it not follow that classes themselves can be classified in terms of their sameness?

Then, we should be able to rank classes in terms of sameness and difference, and if that is so should we not be able to have a class that includes all the other classes as its members?

Then it follows, doesn't it, that since all things fit into classes that can be ordered in terms of their sameness and difference, that everything can be ordered? And, since that order can express degrees of difference, does it not follow that everything and the classes of everything can be ranked to the degree of their sameness, that is, in a hierarchy?

Reflecting on what has been said, would you not agree that if two things are the same in every respect, there would then be no way to distinguish one from the other? Well, if that is true, wouldn't that mean that there really is only *one* thing not *two*, and so it would be proper to say that if things are truly identical, having no difference between them, they would be one, not two? Well, then can we say that since there are things, each of them must be the same in some respect and different in some respect from everything else. And the sameness shared by things establishes them in a class among many hierarchically arranged classes.

Then, everything is related to everything else in the universe by way of sameness and difference since between any two things in the universe there is, at least, one sameness and one difference. Clearly, since there are no things that are so different that neither samenesses nor differences can be detected between them, then, each thing in the universe possesses a uniqueness while sharing some commonness and otherness with all other things. When there is a sameness among classes they can be classed in the same class, or we can say that classes that share some sameness are *similar.*

Everything in the universe can be a member of some class including the class of the classes of everything. Clearly, it follows, in principle, that it is possible to contrast either similar or dissimilar classes and the members of a class in respect to either their sameness or difference. When comparisons, then, are made between similar classes and within the terms of each class we call those classes *similar ratios.* An ordered pair of similar ratios occurs when the particular order of the terms in each ratio are the same. And, since the least number of terms in a comparison is two, the minimum number of terms and ratios in an analogy are two.

Comparisons between inverted members of similar ratios generate likenesses called *similes*. The nature of likeness lies in distinguishing a sameness in sets or classes whose terms are similarly ordered. For while the similar set of relations exists within each ratio of an analogy, they, of course, have their own uniqueness within each ratio; but their sameness can be grasped by another kind of similarity, and that is in how they *function*. This similarity of function can be expressed in the idea of *likeness*. And since likeness is a kind of similarity derived from inverted terms of similar ratios, it presupposes the existence of a prior order, a hierarchically arranged order.

We find in Plato that he describes the bond of likeness as a property that is carried from one ratio to another, a property that turns about upon itself and shapes a way of seeing that neither had alone so that he can say that analogy has a property to express likeness through itself. The name for this likeness is, of course, derived from the invertendo form of analogy. Thus, it functions, as it were, between two terms carrying an element from one term to another creating what both share but neither has alone. Consider:

"The fog was like a comforting cloak of obscurity."

or

"Her mind had a rare clarity to it like the radiance of a clear winter night."

And while not expressing a sameness alone, it expresses a similarity called Likeness, and this combines both in a way that sends echoes back to each of the terms.

The idea of likeness is a principle idea in metaphysics. The study of metaphysics requires that you allow yourself to explore ideas in a new way. It is said to be simple and difficult. Simple because if you reflect on each of the points in a metaphysical exploration they should be simple. But the simple for the wise may not be the simple for the fool. The fool's simplicity might become wise if he would endure the study of the simple, but the fool's foolishness is in believing that doing that is foolish.

Let us return to the idea of likeness and discuss it as Proclus does in his *Commentary to Plato's Parmenides*. Well, now to begin, would you not agree, that unless things could become like another there would be no likeness among things? For if things *have become, are,* or *will become* like other things, the property of likeness must have prior existence. Or, stated another way, whatever is used existed prior to its use. The condition for likeness must exist, then, for likenesses to exist. Further, when anything becomes like the thing that it seeks then the condition of likeness makes it possible for it to be like its model.

Anything that becomes better or improves in any way does so by becoming like the thing it becomes like. All the making, copying, or producing of anything is making it *like* the model of that thing. All things like another thing are so because of the condition that made that likeness possible. As long as that condition persists or is maintained then we can say that it is the single tie that joins and holds all things together. Surely, when things become like they share a common likeness, and they also have that commonness that joins them together. But each thing becoming like a model becomes more like its ideal or archetype. For the being of each thing is defined by its likeness to the intelligible model, and it's through being like its idea that each is what it truly is. Then, likeness is the factor that perfects the being of each since perfection comes to each when it becomes like its intelligible form. As a consequence of likeness being the condition for things becoming like, we can say that all this perfecting of such things is conditioned by likeness.

The likeness of things in similar classes is expressed in and through analogy, and it is this factor that is called the natural property of analogy. Then, anything made or created presupposes the condition of likeness. Indeed, since God's creation is often spoken of as being like himself we can say the condition of likeness made it possible for the universe and man to be akin to himself. But this is saying, is it not, that the "supreme originating cause of the universe" is the principle of analogy? And, again, does it not follow that this principle must be logically prior to creation? And, once again, does not the principle of analogy also allow and make possible the condition for linking or bonding together whatever is? Plato grasped this in a superb manner when he said in the *Timaeus:*

> *"And the most beautiful of bonds is that which most perfectly unites into one both itself and the things which it binds together, and to effect this in the most beautiful manner is the natural property of analogy."* (31C)

However, must there not be a model and something produced like it for likeness to exist? Then, model, copy, and likeness coming together are required for any creation. Now, if the model is nothing other than God, then in the act of creation God looks to himself in producing the creation. But that which he looks to as a model must itself have some kind of existence or mode of being, must it not? Now, if that is the model which we could call the mind of God—the divine intelligence— then whatever was the cause or the condition for that must be called the creator of the model, must it not? So then, in review, can we say there is God, God who produced the intelligence, God who reflects on himself in creating and the creation itself? Further, is not the reflecting on the model God contemplating the divine intelligence? Then, these different ideas of God, or moments of creative processes, are collectively the Idea of divine creation which must have an existence prior to creation. Further, since these ideas are presupposed for the creation, maintenance, and dissolution of the universe they are the necessary condition for it. For as the maker produces and creates what is evolving, the conditions for that evolution must have a prior existence. For since the suspension of the conditions for evolving would bring an end to the universe, the factors necessary for its evolving must remain in place. Thus, these ideas that are necessary for creation can be said to gain their continued existence from the continued reflection of God on the Idea of creation—which is to say God's continued contemplation of the Idea of creation sustains and directs the universe. Therefore, we can call this Idea in the mind of God the first creation and the universe the second, and both are sustained by the creative contemplation of God.

The first creation's origin is God, and since it is an Idea, God must be the source of the existence of mind—if not God itself. Again, since it is an Idea it must contain within itself all that is necessary for the creation, and that being the case it must either have or will have parts, i. e., a manyness. The Idea we can say is One but its unity of parts presents a oneness. Another word for unity is oneness, and oneness is called the property or quality of the One. Surely, that oneness, or unity, of the Idea must contain within itself, at least implicitly, all that later develops from it. But if it is a one that has parts, then the many parts would make it a one-of-many-parts which would be a unity of a many and not a pure one. The One itself then is the source of Oneness, and if the Idea of Oneness stands to the Idea of Creation, so the One must stand to God. For a pure One must be such as to have no parts but the cause and source of oneness. Further, would it not follow that the One can not be identical with anything, nor the same with anything, nor similar to any class of things, but the source of them all?

But is this not curious—this exchanging and even mixing together the idea of God and his creation with the One and the Many? Well, you become a theologian when you use the idea of God and creation; and you become a metaphysician with the use of the One and the Many; and when you mix them you become both. The advantage of the metaphysical lies in developing a system of thought—a metaphysics—that is implicit in our thought and which can be unfolded in and through understanding and presented in language; this is called the functioning of the *logos*. Can we say that a pure idea of One can be what a pure idea of God is? But the idea of One, a pure One seems empty of all that would be needed to call a God a God. Yet many of the ancient Greek philosophers argued that a pure One would necessarily have to be Good. What kind of reasoning could support such a claim?

Consider: The idea of God's goodness is a matter of belief, but to try to *understand* that rather than simply *believe* it is the task of metaphysics. And to achieve that requires explaining in what way the One and the Good are identical.

Analogy

Let us examine one of the propositions that Proclus developed to express the idea that the One and the Good are identical. But before we explore this let me put a few questions to you:

Would you say that there must be something that makes things whole? And something that holds together the parts of whatever is?

And if it did do that, would it not make things into a one?

And when it loses that unity, does not decay, separation, and dispersal set in?

If there is this idea of oneness, does that mean there must be a One from which it derived its quality of oneness?

If we can speak of things becoming unified then to that degree we can say they gain a oneness but does this mean that oneness has some kind of a presence that perfects as it unifies?

Would you say that if anything can bring about the wholeness of anything, you would be willing to call it good? Would that also be something that perfects whatever gains some perfection?

Proclus' 13ᵀᴴ Proposition

Now, let us consider a translation of Proclus's 13th Proposition made by friend and colleague, Barbara Stecker. Notice the first part is the statement that is set out to be proven; this is *the statement of the proposition.*

I. *Every good unifies what shares in it, all union is good, and the Good is identical with the One.*

The second part, following the introduction, explores the Idea of the Good and its relationship to the Idea of the One.

the bond

II. *If, indeed the Good brings about the wholeness of all beings (on this account desire begins in all) but what makes whole and holds together the being (ουσια) of each is the One (by the One indeed all are made whole and dispersal deprives each of being/ουσια) then the Good for those it is present to brings completion as one and holds together according to the union.*

The third part explores the One and its relationship to the Good.

III. *And if the One is what brings together and holds together beings, it* [perfects] *each according to its presence. Then in this way to unify* unificat. *self is good for all. But if union is in itself good, and the Good is what unifies, the unqualified Good and the unqualified One is identical, at once unifying and making beings good.*
① ②

The fourth part deals with what follows if the second and third part are rejected.

IV. *Indeed, whenever there are those that in some way fall away from the good these are at the same time deprived of sharing in the One, and when those come to have no share (portion) in the One, they are deprived of the Good in the same way.*

And, finally, the fifth part restates what has been discussed.

if beings fall away from the Good, they don't share in the One. If they don't share in the One, they don't share in the Good.

V.   *Therefore,* goodness is union, *and union is goodness and the Good is the One, and the One is primarily the Good.*

To explore this kind of reasoning further it is important to read Proclus's *Elements of Theology* and his *Commentary on Plato's Parmenides.* If you find this challenging, you will enjoy the life of the mind; and while no one may know where your search will end, there is little doubt you will find your life richer and more profound by taking the trip. Thanks for going to the end of this little exercise. I wish you good fortune on your present and future quest.

MORE QUESTIONS FOR YOUR REFLECTION

There are three acts to the play, *Is It All Relative?* and in each of these acts the characters—Joseph, Elea, and Harry—discuss many subjects.

Who among them would you say is interpreting? On what issues?

As you consider each of the three acts and reflect on what is said in each, you get a sense of how the characters interact with one another and whether or not they themselves went through any kind of change. Considering the conclusions they came to, please answer the following:

Do you think any of them changed as a result of what they went through? What would you say influenced you most when you made that conclusion? And do you think you could find a line or two from the play to support your point of view?

If there is a change, who changes and who does not? What would it mean if one could go through such a talk without going through any kind of change? Why?

What is it to be *philosophically pregnant*? What are the signs of being philosophically pregnant? Who would you say was pregnant? What signs do they exhibit of being philosophically pregnant? What is *philosophical midwifery*?

Could you say something about the positions the characters of the play held in respect to, say, religion, history, or philosophy—or anything else that occurs to you? Like ecology? Or models? Belief? Myth?

Say, what is it like to understand in this way? Is it a way of understanding without an object? What is understanding, then?

131

REFERENCES AND SUGGESTED READING

Aland, Kurt. *Synopsis of the Four Gospels: Greek-English*. Stuttgart: German Bible Society (Biblia-Druck), 1971.

Brehier, Emile. *The Hellenic Age*. trans. Joseph Thomas. Chicago: The University of Chicago Press, 1963.

Buchanan, Scott. *Poetry and Mathematics*. New York: Keystone Books, J. B. Lippincott, Co., 1957. A fine study of the common roots of poetry and math.

___, *Symbolic Distance, Psyche Miniatures*. London: Kegan Paul, 1932. A speculative work, insightful and imaginative.

Bultmann, Rudolph. *The New Testament and Mythology*. ed. H. Werner Bartsch. Vol. 1 of *Kerygma and Myth: A Theological Debate*. London: The Society for Promoting Christian Knowledge, London, England. Naperville, IL, 1953.

Cornford, Francis M. *Plato's Theory of Knowledge. Part One*. Indianapolis, IN: The Bobs-Merrill Company, 1976.

Gibbon. *The Decline and Fall of the Roman Empire*. Ed. Dero A. Saunders. New York: The Viking Press, 1960.

Hastings, J. *Encyclopedia of Religion and Ethics*. New York: Abners, 1958.(see Von Dobschutz' article on "Interpretation," p.390.)

Heath, Thomas. *Euclid: The Elements*. 3 vols. Annapolis: St. John's College Press, 1947. Note that Books V & VII are the books on proportion.

Hengel, Martin. *Judaism and Hellenism*. Vols. 1& 2. trans. John Bowden. Philadelphia: Fortress Press, 1981.

Huizianga, Johan. *Homo Ludens: A Study of the Play Element in Culture*. Boston: Beacon Press, 1950.

Lawlor, Robert. *Philosophy and Practice: Sacred Geometry*. Thames and Hudson, 1989. This truly beautiful work with over 200 illustrations explores analogy and its references to the more profound philosophical movements through geometry and analogy and also has a wonderful bibliography.

Lonergan, Bernard, J. I. *Insight*. New York: Harper and Row, 1978. There is an interesting section on the dialectic, myth, allegory, and analogy. For an insight into the mean analogy and its geometrical representation read this insightful work.

Maccoby, Hyam. *The Mythmaker*. San Francisco: Harper & Row, 1986.

McClain, Ernest C. *The Myth Of Invariance*. Nicolas Hays, Ltd., 1976. This work relates the Hindu *Rig Veda* and Plato through music and mathematics.

Otto, Walter F. *The Homeric Gods*. trans. Moses Hadas. Boston: Beacon Press, 1954.

Palmer, P. *Hermeneutics: Interpretation Theory in Schleiemacher, Dilthey, Heidegger, and Gadamer*. Evanston, Illinois: Northwestern University Press, 1969.

Philo. trans. F. H. Colson & G. H. Whitaker. 10 vols. The Loeb Classical Library. Cambridge: Harvard University Press.

Plato. *The Dialogues of Plato*. trans. B. Jowett. New York: Random House, 1937.

Plato. *The Great Dialogues of Plato*. trans. W.H.D. Rouse. NewYork: Mentor Press, Signet Press, 1956.

Plato. *Republic*. trans. Paul Shorey. vols. 1 & 2. 1978. The Loeb Classical Library. Cambridge: Harvard University Press, 1978.

Plato. *Theaetetus and Sophist*. trans. H. N. Fowler. The Loeb Classical Library. Cambridge: Harvard University Press, 1921.

Plato. *Timaeus and Critias*. trans. Thomas Taylor. New York: Pantheon Books, 1952. (with a foreword by R. Catesby Taliaferro) All of Plato's dialogues are recommended, but the Timaeus is central to the study of analogy and the foreword by Taliaferro is most interesting and thought provoking.

Smith, Huston. *Beyond the Post-Modern Mind*. Wheaton, Illinois: The Theosophical Publishing House, 1989.

The Torah, the Five Books of Moses. Philadelphia: The Jewish Publication Society of America, 1962.

"You! You are a man! You have a VOICE. Speak your mind, for meaningful sounds have been awaited since immeasurable time. Give voice to the vision of Man. And through continual questioning and reflection may you polish to a brilliance that which illuminates the soul and so ends the dark silence of the ages."

A. Finsky

The body text for *Is It All Relative* was typeset using *TimesNewRomanPS* by
Adobe®

Address comments and questions to:

Hyparxis Press
2172 Pacific Avenue
Costa Mesa, CA 92627-3912.

We appreciate your interest in what we publish.

NOTES:

NOTES: